The Engineering Student Survival Guide

McGraw-Hill's *BEST*—**B**ASIC
ENGINEERING SERIES AND TOOLS

Bertoline: *Introduction to Graphics Communications for Engineers*

Burghardt: *Introduction to Engineering Design and Problem Solving*

Chapman: *Introduction to Fortran 90/95*

Donaldson: *The Engineering Student Survival Guide*

Eide et al.: *Introduction to Engineering Design*

Eide et al.: *Introduction to Engineering Problem Solving*

Eisenberg: *A Beginner's Guide to Technical Communication*

Gottfried: *Spreadsheet Tools for Engineers: Excel '97 Version*

Greenlaw and Hepp: *Introduction to the Internet for Engineers*

Mathsoft's Student Edition of Mathcad 7.0

Palm: *Introduction to MATLAB for Engineers*

Pritchard, Mathcad: *A Tool for Engineering Problem Solving*

Smith: *Project Management and Teamwork*

Tan and D'Orazio: *C Programming for Engineering and Computer Science*

The Engineering Student Survival Guide

K. Donaldson

Boston   Burr Ridge, IL   Dubuque, IA   Madison, WI   New York   San Francisco   St. Louis
Bangkok   Bogotá   Caracas   Lisbon   London   Madrid
Mexico City   Milan   New Delhi   Seoul   Singapore   Sydney   Taipei   Toronto

WCB/McGraw-Hill

*A Division of The **McGraw·Hill** Companies*

THE ENGINEERING STUDENT SURVIVAL GUIDE

This book is printed on acid-free paper.

2 3 4 5 6 7 8 9 0 DOC/DOC 9 3 2 1 0 9

ISBN 0-07-228647-4

Vice president/Editor-in-Chief: *Kevin T. Kane*
Publisher: *Thomas Casson*
Executive editor: *Eric M. Munson*
Developmental editor: *Holly Stark*
Marketing manager: *John T. Wannemacher*
Project manager: *Kimberly Schau*
Production associate: *Debra R. Benson*
Freelance design coordinator: *JoAnne Schopler*
Cover design and interior illustrations: *Daniel Kim*
Compositor: *Electronic Publishing Services, Inc.*
Typeface: *10/12 Palantino*
Printer: *R. R. Donnelley & Sons Company*

CREDITS

Page vii: Courtesy of The Herbert Hoover Presidential Library; **Page 30:** Courtesy United Media; **Page 32:** Courtesy Derek Reamon, Doctoral Student, Stanford University; **Page 43:** From *The Bulletin of Vanderbilt University 1994/5 Undergraduate Catalog,* reproduced by permission of Vanderbilt University; **Page 57:** From *Webster's College Dictionary,* ed. Robert B. Costello, copyright © 1991 by Random House, Inc.; **Page 85:** Excerpt from *Linear Algebra and Its Applications,* Third Edition by Gilbert Strang, copyright © 1988 by Harcourt Brace & Company, reproduced by permission of the publisher; **Page 131:** Excerpt from *Genius: The Life and Science of Richard Feynman* by James Gleick, copyright © 1993, Vintage Books, Pantheon Books, a Division of Random House, Inc.

Library of Congress Cataloging-in-Publication Data

Donaldson, Krista.
    The engineering student survival guide / Krista Donaldson.
        p.   cm. — (McGraw-Hill's BEST—basic engineering series and tools)
    Includes bibliographical references (p.).
    ISBN 0-07-228647-4
    1. Engineering—Study and teaching (Higher)—United States.
    2. Engineering students—United States. 3. College student orientation—United States.   I. Title. II. Series.
    T73.D66   1999
    620'.0071' 173—dc21   98-38255

http://www.mhhe.com

Foreword

Engineering educators have had long-standing debates over the content of introductory freshman engineering courses. Some schools emphasize computer-based instruction, some focus on engineering analysis, some concentrate on graphics and visualization, while other emphasize hands-on design. Two things, however, appear certain: no two schools do exactly the same thing, and at most schools, the introductory engineering courses frequently change from one year to the next. In fact, the introductory engineering courses at many schools have become a smorgasbord of different topics, some classical and others closely tied to computer software applications. Given this diversity in content and purpose, the task of providing appropriate text material becomes problematic, since every instructor requires something different.

McGraw-Hill has responded to this challenge by creating a series of modularized textbooks for the topics covered in most first-year introductory engineering courses. Written by authors who are acknowledged authorities in their respective fields, the individual modules vary in length, in accordance with the time typically devoted to each subject. For example, modules on programming languages are written as introductory-level textbooks, providing material for an entire semester of study, whereas modules that cover shorter topics such as ethics and technical writing provide less material, as appropriate for a few weeks of instruction. Individual instructors can easily combine these modules to conform to their particular courses. Most modules include numerous problems and/or projects, and are suitable for use within an active-learning environment.

The goal of this series is to provide the educational community with text material that is timely, affordable, of high quality, and flexible in how it is used. We ask that you assist us in fulfilling this goal by letting us know how well we are serving your needs. We are particularly interested in knowing what, in your opinion, we have done well, and where we can make improvements or offer new modules.

Byron S. Gottfried
Consulting Editor
University of Pittsburgh

ENGINEERING

It is a great profession. There is the fascination of watching a figment of the imagination emerge through the aid of science to a plan on paper. Then it moves to realization in stone or metal or energy. Then it brings homes and jobs to men. Then it elevates the standards of living and adds to the comforts of life. That is the engineer's high privilege.

The great liability of the engineer compared to men of other professions is that his works are out in the open where all can see them. His acts, step by step, are in hard substance. He cannot argue them into thin air or blame the judge like lawyers. He cannot, like the politicians, screen his shortcomings by blaming his opponents and hope the people will forget. The engineer simply cannot deny he did it.

On the other hand, unlike the doctor his life is not a life among the weak. Unlike the soldier, destruction is not his purpose. Unlike the lawyer, quarrels are not his daily bread. To the engineer falls the job of clothing the bare bones of science with life, comfort, and hope. No doubt as years go by the people forget which engineer did it, even if they ever knew. Or some politician put his name on it. Or they credit it to some promoter who used other people's money . . . But the engineer looks back at the unending stream of goodness which flows from his successes with satisfaction that few professionals may know. And the verdict of his fellow professionals is all the accolade he wants.

—Herbert Hoover, American Mining Engineer
and thirty-first U. S. President (1874–1964)

Brief Contents

Contents

Preface

This isn't a book about how to get along with your roommate or how to balance your college budget (hey—you're an engineer, a calculator is never far away). I've tried to avoid phrases like (ugh!) *time management, goal setting,* and *finding yourself.* The assumption has been made that you have found yourself and an engineering program for yourself. Less lofty and more useful topics will be covered. Engineering students are perceived to have a heavier workload than the average student. That perception is, well . . . pretty much correct, but the perception that we have to give up our social lives is simply not true.

What this book *is* about is how to learn as much as you can, get choice grades, and still have fun while pursuing an engineering degree. You will find strategies to ace tests, navigate your way around campus without looking and feeling too much like a freshman, learn to love your computer in times of cyber-crisis, and pull through end-of-the-quarter slams in ways that are specific to *engineers.* Did you notice that we always get left out of college handbooks? It must be that we are just too intimidating.

Enough said. Prefaces are usually a drag. Much of this is common sense and ever more is I-wish-someone-had-told-me-this-when-I-was-a-freshman. I can't say I always follow my own advice, so take only what you like and have fun.

K. D.

The Engineering Student Survival Guide

CHAPTER 1

Let's Take a Shot at Defining Success

So it's all in how you define it.

Right? Sort of. As you pass through the hallowed academic hallways, others will also get a shot at defining your success with grades, friendships, and respect. Even so, ultimately *you* define your own success by setting your own expectations, limits, standards, and goals.

You've chosen your school, decided to be an engineer—or at least get an engineering education!—and even may have selected your discipline. Mom and Dad are proud. Your high school or junior college math and sciences teachers are pleased. Your older (nonengineering) friends already at university are impressed—"You know engineering is pretty hard . . . Wow."

Engineers are admired. Engineers are cool. There is a reason:

Engineering *is* hard.

You will at times (like during the 2:00 A.M. millionth attempt at debugging a computer science assignment) curse the person who said that the college years are the best years of one's life. Many late nights aren't spent partying, but working on problem sets (while your friends may be partying). Engineering students typically have longer exams than other majors and more of them. Everything you learn builds on itself.

To become an engineer (admired and cool):

You must work (very hard).

Those two points are the most important things to understand up front. The good thing is that the harder you think you have to work, the less you will realize it. Not overly comforting, eh? College isn't any less fun because you have more work to do. The more work you do, the more you appreciate your fun times.

College definitely shouldn't be all work. Given that and talking to lots of folks in and out of school, a survey says (in "Family Feud" style) that a truly successful undergraduate engineering experience requires at least the following:

- ☺ A solid understanding of what was taught to you (which is hopefully reflected by your grades).
- ☺ Confidence at graduation that you are academically prepared for your next adventure whether it is in the work world or graduate school.
- ☺ Great friends.
- ☺ More "growing experiences" than you felt were needed or to which you were entitled.
- ☺ Awesome memories with which to torture your grandchildren.
- ☺ Time and opportunity to develop completely random interests.

The above goals may seem long range and abstract, but they come easily if you can maintain the daily LSS (Life, School, and Sanity) Balance and achieve the Ben Balance. The LSS and Ben Balances are discussed in Chapter 10, but for now that means simply that you are pleased with yourself and your surroundings on a daily basis.

So, back to success and its definition. Personal success is what makes you happy, whether it is a slick free body diagram, a perfect score on a problem set, a computer science program that *finally* works, or being able to go to bed at a decent hour before a big test. Love what you do—or at least like most of it. Engineering is cool.

> *Science can amuse and fascinate us all,*
> *but it is engineering that changes the world.*
> —Isaac Asimov
> Russian-American biochemist
> and writer (b. 1920)

CHAPTER 2

Before You Go— Preparation for Education?

The best preparation you can give yourself is time and confidence. Avoiding important science classes such as Physics until you get to college will prove hazardous to your health. It will be both time-consuming and stressful as you try to keep up with your classmates and the material. On top of that, the introductory science courses facing a freshman engineer are geared to be deliberately grueling to eliminate struggling students (what upperclassmen call "weed-outs"); so the workload will be heavy, the tests get exponentially harder, and, although the covered concepts are familiar, everything seems more difficult. Engineers also have a rigid schedule and an arm's-length list of requirements needed to graduate in the usual four or five years. In fact, dropping just *one* class can force you into summer school—or out of the social scene and into the library for a semester in the hope of making up the units. Taking a class at a community college for college credit while still in high school or during the summer can free you up to take a lighter course load or to devote more time to a demanding class during the regular school year.

FOUR WAYS TO GIVE YOURSELF A HEAD START BEFORE COLLEGE

1. Take as much math and science as you can.

Most of the nonscience and nonmath classes that the National Society of Professional Engineers recommends for future engineers are the *same* classes required to receive your high school diploma:

- ☺ Four years of English.
- ☺ Three years of social studies.
- ☺ One to two years of arts or humanities.
- ☺ Two to three years of foreign languages.

So you've already got that covered!

> ☞ **To like engineering,** you don't necessarily have to *like* math or the sciences, but you should be confident in your ability to think analytically and solve problems.

To receive a bachelor's degree, engineering students must complete at least all math classes up to and including Differential Equations. To reach Differential Equations, you must complete Algebra I and II, Geometry, Trigonometry, Calculus I, II , and III (differential calculus, integral calculus, multivariable calculus, respectively). Some schools also require classes in Linear Algebra and Statistics. Fortunately or unfortunately (depending on how much you have paid attention in math class), the material taught in your required math classes is frequently used to explain engineering derivations, laws, proofs, and problem sets. Trig functions become second nature to the engineering student.

All engineers must have a good grounding in the sciences: physics, chemistry, and, depending on your major, biology. The better you understand these subjects *before* going into college, the better prepared you will be to handle the accelerated pace of your college professors.

2. Get as many advanced placement (AP)[1] credits under your belt in the arts, humanities, and social sciences as possible.

Of course, *all* AP credits are an asset. If your goal is get your degree in the shortest amount of time possible, then use all your AP credits to get ahead. But if you know you have four or five years to complete your degree, then go ahead and take the standard introductory science and math classes offered to engineering students at your university. The reasons for doing this are quite simple. First, most of the students in your classes will be premed, science majors, or other engineers; thus, the material focuses on the subject areas that will *best* prepare you for your engineering education in the following years. Second, many students who opt to "retake" math and science classes find that these courses cover useful, unfamiliar material and with little work also pad their first semester report card very nicely.

On the other hand, filling up your arts and crafts—oops . . . arts and humanities!—requirements with advanced placement credits gives you room in your schedule to enroll in more interesting free electives (The Beatles and Beethoven! Windsurfing!) that may be unique to your university.

3. If you know you need to catch up in a subject or area, try to do so before you go to college.

Maybe you aren't fully confident in your math ability or perhaps you were a few painful points short of the minimum on your college placement exam to get into a required English class. Don't waste precious free electives taking the

---

[1]Advanced Placement courses are college-level classes offered at some U.S. high schools. The standardized exam at the end of the course is graded on a scale of 1 to 5, with individual universities setting their own standards to grant credit. High schools that do not offer AP classes may have honors classes that are equivalent in level and depth of material covered, but do not directly result in college credit.

remedial classes at university to get caught up—check out a grammar guide from your local library or take a prep class at the community college; *then* retake the placement exam. Many community colleges and high schools have evening classes and accelerated summer classes that are perfect cram courses for instilling academic confidence. A strong start at university is more than good grades; it also establishes self-assurance in your academic abilities.

4. Consider any high school electives that might give a glimpse of engineering.

Universities tend to make the baseline assumption that their freshmen students have had only high school–level math (Analytical Geometry, Trig, and Pre-Calc) and science (Physics, Chem, and Bio). Many high schools hope to better prepare students for college and industry by offering classes in Engineering Technology, Machine Shop, and Computer Programming. Classes like these and others give you a jump-start with exposure to the terms, processes, and methodologies that you will encounter as an engineering student.

GREAT GOING-TO-COLLEGE GIFT IDEAS FOR YOURSELF (OR, GOOD TOOLS TO BRING)

What do engineers need that other college students don't? We need pretty much the same things our nonengineering peers require, except *maybe* a smarter calculator and a real computer (not the wimpy word-processing kind), *and* both of these items can probably wait a semester or two. You will definitely need the checked items that follow during your college years and beyond. The unchecked items are useful to have, but perhaps not a definite need.

- ☑ *Dictionary.* Any college edition will do.
- ☑ *Thesaurus.* Although many word-processing software packages have a built-in thesaurus, the book-form college edition is much more comprehensive. It is well worth its weight after the first late-night, five-page paper brain-fry. Suggestion: Any college edition.
- ☐ *Desk reference set.* If you just graduated from high school, it is very likely that you received one of these lovely little brown sets as a graduation gift. The set includes a spelling dictionary, grammar guide, random facts book (conversion tables are a definite asset), mini thesaurus, dictionary, and maybe an atlas and a few other things. Everything in the set will be useful at least once.
- ☑ *Paper writing/documentation guide.* Engineers still have to write a few papers! Not to worry—they are usually not long ones. Suggestions: *MLA Style Manual* (Modern Language Association of America), and *Elements of Style* (William Strunk and E. B. White).
- ☐ *Compasses, rulers, . . . any handy mathematical and graphical tools.* Believe it or not, engineers do a lot of sketching when illustrating ideas, designs, free body diagrams, best-fit curves, and flowcharts. Even a template with different sized circles and squares saves time.
- ☐ *Any old* useful *math or science textbooks or formula sheets.* In your senior year at university, you'll find you are still hauling out the freshmen

physics book to retrieve the formula for a sphere's surface area, or a decrepit chemistry book because you can't remember some basic stoichiometry for a combustion process calculation. Sometimes old textbooks have clearer explanations of concepts or of useful example problems.

☑ *Scientific calculator.* See the next page for more on the engineer's best friend.

☐ *Graphing and/or programmable calculator.* Wow! These things are the bomb! Graphing makes math homework sets easy to check and solve. Programming saves countless hours of time calculating roots to polynomials, solving the determinants of matrices, and so on. If you decide to purchase a really good one, wait a few semesters to talk to upperclassmen and find out what works best for you.

Whichever calculator you choose, pick one that has complex number capabilities (electrical engineers, take note!), integrates, isolates variables, . . . in short, meets *your* needs. Suggestions: Hewlett-Packard (HP), Texas Instrument (TI), and Casio.

⚠ **Watch out!** Nice calculators have been known to disappear. Carve your driver's license number on the back or personally vandalize it in some other way that identifies your ownership.

☐ *Answering machine or voice mail.* A few years ago this would be a luxury; now having an anwering machine or voice mail is virtually a necessity for college students—especially engineers. Engineers are notorious for their late night phone networks through which they excange information: answer comparisons, strategies in tackling tough problem sets, and stressed and sometimes profane opinions of their major and its workload. And engineering professors are sometimes known for having trouble finding a room for help sessions, giving incorrect answers for an assigned problem set, and even postponing a test date when a student coup appears to be looming. Whether you use an answering machine or voice mail to screen calls or to save them, it gets use.

☐ *Computer.* Should you bring a computer? If you can, you definitely should. Owning your own computer saves time going to and from the university computer lab, and from being at the mercy of lab hours, crowds, rules ("WHADD'YA MEAN I CAN'T BRING MY COFFEE IN HERE?!"), broken printers, and viruses. At some universities, engineering students *must* bring their own computer. If you are undecided, wait a semester or two to see whether a personal computer is a necessity; that way you will have a better idea of what model suits you best. Used computers are a less expensive option. Suggestion: See "Buying a Computer—Advice for the Wise" for some ideas on page 13.

More gifts to acquire if you bring a computer:

☐ *Backups of all software.* Bring everything, crashes happen!
☐ *Software reference manuals.*
☐ *Power bar with surge protector.* Computers can protect themselves against internal power surges, but not against external surges from beyond the wall. A five- or six-dollar surge protector is cheap insurance!

There Are Two Breeds of the Engineer's Best Friend

There are two formats that high-end calculators use for computation: standard arithmetic and the mysterious RPN.

Standard arithmetic is what most calculators use: Computation is executed as it is entered and appears on the screen. For example, if you want to multiply the sum of 2 and 5 by 8, you would have to use parentheses because of the order of operations:

$$(2 + 5) \times 8$$

Standard arithmetic would allow you to enter the operands (numbers), operators (+ and ×), and parentheses in the same order you might write it.

RPN originated with a Polish mathematical logician named Jan Lukasiewicz who in 1951 wrote a book showing that mathematical expressions could be specified without worrying about parentheses. He did this by placing the operators after the operands (postfix notation). Lukasiewicz would write the above expression as:

$$8\ 5\ 2 + \times$$

While this postfix notation looks pretty confusing, many engineers swear by its efficiency. Lukasiewicz also had a prefix notation that was dubbed "Polish Notation" in honor of him. When Hewlett-Packard (HP) adapted the postfix notation to its calculators, they dubbed it "Reverse Polish Notation"—RPN—also in his honor.

☐ *Three-pronged extension cord.* If you don't use this for your computer, you can use it for the microwave or something else.

☐ Extra *phone cord* for modem hookup or *cables* for ethernet.

☐ *Antivirus, disk recovery software* for protecting your computer and your sanity. Still, check first to see if your university has a site license for any software so that students can download it for free.

☐ *Printer, paper, ink cartridges,* and a *controller box* (if you share a printer with your roommate).

A HEADS-UP ON HOUSING

On-campus university housing is usually run as a lottery: You submit your ranked list of residence choices, cross your fingers, and wait to be notified how lucky (or unlucky) you are. Below are just a few things to consider when the time comes to find housing or finalize your preferred dorm list:

☺ If you are bringing a computer with a modem or ethernet, try to snag a room with high-speed data hookup lines. Older dorms are often not wired for this.

☺ If you aren't bringing a computer, how close is the closest computer lab? Is there one in your dorm? Or will you have to trek across campus?

☺ How close are the science labs and libraries? Some evening laboratory classes are not finished until well after dark. Besides the important issues of safety and possible hypothermia in winter, how far do you want to walk or bike home?

Hi there! Hope you don't mind...I took the bottom bunk.

If living on campus is not an option, you may have other considerations such as transportation, parking (how close and how expensive), traffic, and proximity to engineering buildings. However, whether you will be residing on campus or off, you will save time and effort if you allow yourself as much accesss as possible to your school and its resources.

BUYING A COMPUTER—ADVICE TO THE WISE

You're thinking about purchasing a computer and aren't really sure exactly what model you might need compared with the model your older sister (the history major) has, whether you need a computer at all, and, if so, how to begin to start the search. First things first, you'll need to do a little research.

Five Questions for the Potential Computer Purchaser

1. Do you *really* need a computer?

Purchasing a computer is a huge endeavor in terms of time and money spent. To determine if you will need a personal computer for your personal use in your own personal space, consider the following: *What are the campus computing facilities like?* You can figure that out by asking even more questions:

Q: How many computer labs are located on campus?
Q: Where are they located (i.e., how close to your living quarters)?
Q: How early do the computer labs open? Are they open all night? (This is important.)

Q: Are printers readily accessible? Is printing free or are there printing charges?

Q: Do all of the labs have engineering software?

Q: Are computers generally available or are there frequent waiting lists to get on to one?

Q: Does the guy who works in the computer lab recommend that you buy your own computer?

Q: How tight are your finances?

If you don't already have an engineering contact (your brother's girl-friend's cousin's roommate counts) at your chosen university, find the computer center (it might be called Center for Computing Resources, Computer & Network Services, Computer Help Desk, etc.). Call its information line, look for a web site, or drop in on a computer lab when visiting the campus and look for the brochure or an odd-colored xeroxed handout titled something like "Computing at your University."

Indeed, you have much to think about. To make it a bit easier (or harder), some of the pros and cons in making the decision to take a computer home or to call the computer lab home are given in the following tables.

You Are Monogamous: A Computer to Call Your Own

The GOOD	The Bad	The Ugly
✔ Always available ✔ Can work anytime: day or night ✔ Not at mercy of lab hours, problems, rules, noise ✔ It's in your room, not 10 minutes away ✔ Have choices ✔ More independence ✔ Can check E-mail and do research on the Web from home	✘ Still have to buy software ✘ It loses value ✘ Something else to move at the end of the year ✘ Maintenance is your responsibility	✘✘ The price

You Are Polygamous: A Labful to Love

The GOOD	The Bad	The Ugly
✔ Cost covered by tuition ✔ Lab monitors (and classmates) can help with problems (and problem sets) ✔ Everything you need is there ✔ High quality printers	✘ Even though a computer is available, a software license may not be ✘ No control over noise and distraction level ✘ Can take forever to print	✘✘ Lab full when you badly need a computer ✘✘ Lab may not be open 24 hours

The question really is: Who wouldn't own a computer if they were free? Most students don't own a computer because it is too expensive. And don't forget once you buy the computer, you still have to purchase software, printer, paper, ink cartridges, modem, school-emblazoned mouse pad, aaghh! Below are ways to hang onto your arm and leg.

☺ *Buy a used computer!* Check signs around campus and the student paper.

☺ *Shop smart—compare more than the price.* When considering the various prices of brand-spankin'-new computers, also compare the software packages that would be included with your purchase. How good is the technical support? If you really have time, head for the library and look up individual computer ratings in back issues of consumer magazines (such as *Consumer Reports*) and computer magazines.

☺ *You don't have to buy a printer.* Most universities are networked well enough so that you can send a document to a lab printer over ethernet from your room. If your dorm isn't wired, take files on a disk to print out at the lab on the way to class.

☺ *Software is expensive, BUT there are cheaper student editions of most software.* Remember to take your student I.D.! You will probably be asked to show it when purchasing student editions.

☺ *Start with the basics.* Besides the box, monitor, keyboard, and a few cords, the only other necessary add-ons are a mouse and modem or ethernet capabilities, and they are probably already included.

☺ *How cheap is your university computer store?* University computer stores and bookstores are a good place to buy software (student versions), but they are not usually the cheapest places to purchase computers (think about how much you pay for textbooks!). Instead, head for the magazine rack, purchase a computer magazine or catalog, and order your computer by mail. Another option is to check out the deals on the World Wide Web and order from a reputable web site. If you want to be able to take your new toy home that night, check out price/warehouse clubs for good deals.

If you are still undecided about purchasing a computer, see how the first semester goes without your own computer. It will become evident fairly quickly whether or not you should purchase one.

☞ **Buying a used computer is like buying a car.** Bill (Gates, if you need to know) wants to sell you his used computer. How much did he pay when he bought it new? Why is he selling it? How much did he use it? What for? Does it have a name it likes to go by? Crash a lot? (Any physical signs of possible abuse?) Did it ever have to be repaired? Has the computer ever gotten a virus? Is the software included in the price? Great! Could I get the manuals and software licensing agreements too, please? (Note: It is illegal to sell a computer with software on it unless the original CD-ROM or disks, manuals, and license agreement are included.)

2. Is your university's engineering school mostly PC or Mac compatible?

Once you decide to purchase a computer, this is where you start. Already you've narrowed the field by half. If you have an ambidextrous campus, consider the following:

Macs versus PCs

✔ Power Macs can read both PC and Mac files.

✔ Better for graphical applications.

✔ Tends to be more user friendly.

✘ Tends to crash more often.

✔ More often used in industry.

✔ Greater software availability (games, shareware from the Web, back-of-the-text software).

✔ Faster for your money.

3. How accessible is the mainframe to students in terms of hookup locations and user time?

High-speed transmission and ethernet outlets in dorm rooms mean that your personal computer with a modem can communicate with a university server. Even if you don't have specialized outlets, you can dial up the university system over a phone line with a modem. Good access to the campus computer system allows you to check E-mail, surf and search the Web, monitor school and checking accounts, send virtual postcards, and run programming assignments from the comfort of your room.

4. How much space do you have in your dorm room and car?

Undoubtedly not very much. Should you look for a laptop rather than a desktop computer?

Laptops versus Desktops

✔ Can travel (nice for group projects).

✔ Takes up much less room (key in tiny dorm rooms and at moving time).

✔ Can hook up to another computer (like a lab computer) for printing, monitor use, file exchange.

✘ Add-ons (external drives, etc.) can quickly make a portable computer stationary.

✘ Need to find electrical outlet if working for sufficient amount of time. Batteries do not last very long (about 2.5 hours).

✘ More likely to be stolen.

✔ Larger monitor.

✔ Better keyboard (laptops usually don't have a number pad).

✔ Less likely to get banged up.

✔ Better sound.

✔ Cheaper for memory and speed.

✔ Can keep adding memory cards.

5. Will you be using your computer for anything besides the normal academic and Internet applications (e.g., any plans or aspirations to work on the yearbook staff or become dormitory president)?

This becomes a question of how much hard drive memory will be enough to store standard application programs, games (of course!), bland engineering programs from the back of textbooks, and the desktop publisher needed for the yearbook committee or campaign signs.

SOFTWARE YOU WILL NEED.

Word processing with an equation editor: for example, Microsoft Word or Corel Word Perfect.

Spreadsheet program: for example, Excel, Lotus, Quattro Pro.

Desktop organizer.

Network browser: for example, Netscape Navigator or Internet Explorer.

Virus protection.

Disk recovery software.

SOFTWARE YOU SHOULD WAIT AND SEE TO PURCHASE.

Math programs: for example, Matlab, Mathematica, Mathcad, Maple.

Any extra plotting programs.

Modeling/Sketching/CAD program.

Any extra statistical analysis programs.

Any computer codes, compilers, and so on.

OTHER PROGRAMS YOU WILL ALSO ACCUMULATE.

Games.

Programs that various professors convince you are essential.

Back-of-the-textbook programs.

Goofy things you've downloaded from the Web.

So school stuff alone eats up a lot of storage. When you have a choice between two or more equivalent programs, consider how much disk space will be taken up with each.

How About a Printer to Go with That Computer?

A printer is also a good thing to own. You can print and edit a paper as many times as you'd like without having to queue up in the lab or even having to walk to it. It is convenient. It is relatively cheap. The big drawback of course is that the printer you purchase will most likely not be a laser printer, which is more expensive, heavier, and usually larger than a standard inkjet printer.

Besides, you will have to run over to the lab on a few occasions *anyway* to print out final reports or highly detailed plots when laser quality is required. Just so you know.

If purchasing a printer, pick one that is:

☺ *Easy to maintain.* Load paper in slot and forget about it until you run out of paper again.

☺ *Sleeping-roommate friendly.* Quiet, that is. You will be printing assignments and such during the wee hours of the morning.

☺ *Easily refillable.* Your printer should use standard ink cartridges carried by the university bookstore. Always have an extra ink cartridge on hand; don't wait until the imminent cartridge death stripes show up.

☺ *Compact enough.* Remember your accommodations.

So now you own a computer.

1. Cool.
2. Give it a name because you will be spending a lot of time with him/her/it (you choose that, too).
3. Start a system log. This is simply a list of major changes you make to your computer—things like adding or deleting software, installing memory, reconfiguring your system, and so forth. Make note of the specific change, date, memory used or added, pertinent technical information (serial numbers, tech support toll-free numbers), and where corresponding files are located. Then, when you have a problem with your computer, it should be easy to track down and fix.

CHAPTER 3

Getting Oriented—
Arriving on Campus

It's those bewildering and frantic three or four days before classes start when you are almost finished unpacking and moving in: ORIENTATION. Undoubtedly you will have placement exams to take, registration packets to pick up, financial aid to secure, ice-breaker barbecues, and lectures to attend on campus security, the honor code, dormitory rules—more than you feel you can possibly remember! Enjoy these few days, meet lots of people, and have fun getting acclimated.

> **Some schools have summer orientation.** Many new students meet future roommates there. They also give you a head start on the paperwork and finding your way around campus before the rest of the student body returns to the start of classes.

TEN THINGS TO DO THAT WILL MAKE YOU FEEL LESS LIKE A FRESHMAN WHEN CLASSES START

1. Find out where the offices of the (Engineering) Registrar and student records are located.

If you haven't yet needed to go to either of these two places, you will in the future—to transfer credits, drop classes, order transcripts, and sort out schedule problems. When you do need to go, depending on the time of year and the proximity of the offices, it is sometimes better to call first or take a book with you.

2. Scout out the library and the computer labs. Make a note of the hours they are open.

OK, it is up to you to decide whether to use the library for studying, but you *will* be using the computer lab whether or not you bring your own computer.

Many introductory engineering classes have the course laboratories in the university computer labs. Even if you can complete assignments over the network from your room, it's often easier to simply go to the lab where you have classmates to talk to (and possibly help you) and have full access to the necessary computer programs and treeware (manuals) that your class uses. It is important to note the hours of operation of the library and computer labs; if the lab closes at midnight and you have a program or assignment due at 8:00 A.M. the next morning, you probably won't want to start it at 10:00 or 11:00 P.M. the night before!

3. Locate your classrooms before classes start.

The (often encoded hieroglyphic) acronyms for class locations are listed in the quarter/semester schedule and at some schools on the Web. If your class location is not shown or is "to be announced," call the registrar or the department of the offered course. The numbering and abbreviating of classrooms and buildings can be confusing (The ground floor is the third floor? Is H530 a building or a room? Or both?). So stick a campus map in the cover of one of those stylish see-through binders and enjoy a leisurely walk around campus. When classes start and you join the crowded 10-minute scramble between classes, you'll appreciate your foresight.

4. Buy books early—if you can!

Engineering books are more expensive than almost all the other textbooks for sale in the bookstore. They can put a dent in any collegiate budget and frustrate the new owner. Nevertheless, stopping in early at the bookstore not only ensures that you will get the textbooks you need (underordering is oh so very common), but often you will be given a choice of *new* or the much less expensive *used* books which, depending on how early you get there, are usually in pretty good shape.

Be careful that you are purchasing the correct books for the correct section of your course. Engineering professors almost always use the same edition of the same textbook for all sections, unlike their arts and humanities counterparts, who might assign vastly different texts for different sections of the same course.

⚠ **If you do want to return a textbook, then what?** Most university bookstores have an official last day to return books. Before then, textbooks can generally be returned hassle-free. After that, however, return policies vary from store to store, but many have a good policy if you bring in your drop card[1] and haven't doodled in the book. Returning class packs or course readers[2], on the other hand, is often not so easy. Most course readers are nonrefundable.

---

[1] A card allowing you to drop a class after the semester or quarter drop/add deadline.
[2] Course readers or class packs are a compilation of lecture notes, lab experiments, excerpts from various texts or other sources, old tests, or anything the instructor thinks will serve you best as accompanying material for the course. If your course reader seems expensive for a bundle of photocopied items, much of the cost can probably be attributed to permissions fees.

5. Find out who the deans are (and what they look like).

You could get through four or five years of education and not see or talk to the dean of the School of Engineering, but in case you should run into him or her . . . Additionally, deans' offices frequently offer services to students such as finding tutors, offering study courses for the licensing exam and standardized tests, and listing information on societies and engineering social events. Many universities and colleges have "pic boards" with deans, professors, and department chairs, with a list of their office locations and departmental affiliation(s).

6. Talk to upperclassmen.

Upperclassmen know all: which classes to take in what order, which professors to seek out and which ones to avoid, what to expect from various professors, which pizza place delivers past 1:00 A.M. to the engineering building, which electives they recommend, and so forth.

7. Be prepared for the lifestyle change.

Change is intimidating and (paradoxically) thrilling. For those who went to boarding school, the transition to college may not be a big deal, but for many others having to share a room, actually read a textbook, or purchase an organizer, is something new. The food won't be like home, classes are staggered throughout the day, and you may not get all the sleep or exercise you would like. Finding a balance between what you *need* to do and *want* to do may not happen overnight (or even the first semester), so trust your best judgment and take good care of your health.

New versus Used Textbooks

University bookstores have cornered the engineering textbook market. While it may be simple enough to purchase *Renaissance Literature* or *A History of Economic Thought* at a corner bookstore, it is not so simple finding a book on biomechanical thermodynamics or transport phenomena. Used and new books don't necessarily have to be purchased from the university bookstore. They also can be purchased from upperclassmen, some university societies and organizations, and occasionally at larger schools that have discount academic bookstores.

New

✔ Sturdier—important if you want to keep.

✔ Most up-to-date edition and software available.

✔ Unblemished.

✘ Higher financial loss if book isn't bought back at the end of the semester.

Used

✔ Less expensive.

✔ Past students have already highlighted important notes.

✔ Sometimes answers to problems are written in book.

✘ Sometimes answers written in the book are wrong!

✘ Sometimes missing software.

8. Go to departmental, library, and computer center overviews if they are offered.

Even though a lot of this information can be accessed over the Web, actually going to scheduled library and computer center orientations are key to saving time down the road in locating and accessing information. Learn how library books and periodicals can be tracked down. Can you find them over the Web or through an electronic library database from your room? Computer centers often have handouts on how to access the Internet, send E-mail, and figure out how much disk space students are allowed.

Departmental overviews are helpful when selecting classes and considering majors or minors. Although the thought of going to a lecture in your spare time might not sound very thrilling, the overviews are an excellent opportunity to learn about the specific disciplines, ongoing research (could you be working for NASA your senior year?), internships, the state of the job market, and the personalities in your department.

9. Get your computer account set up.

Now that you know where the computer center is, getting an E-mail account and disk space is just a matter of finding the *right* explanatory handout in the computer lab.

> ⚠ **Yikes!** Be careful when choosing your user name! At most schools, the user name you pick during freshmen orientation stays with you for your entire collegiate career. *Daddio, hotstuff,* and *beer4me* are definitely easy to remember when prowling a cyberspace chatroom, but be aware that that user name will also go on your resume and professors' E-mail lists.

And if you can't find a handout, don't be intimidated. Usually student computer consultants are available to help you out. Accounts can take up to 24 hours to be activated, so don't stress if you followed all the directions but nothing seems to be working.

10. Surf the Web.

Become Web friendly! The World Wide Web is a great resource. Give yourself some time to surf around your school's web site so that you are familiar with what's there. Many university classes now have their own web sites, mailing lists, and news groups. Did you know you can read your calc syllabus, order Peking duck for eight, send virtual or real flowers (depending on your budget) to your hometown honey, and compile a list of all the people with the same last name in the state of Arizona all without leaving your computer?

The Undergrad Engineering Experience

The undergraduate engineering experience is unique to engineers and incomprehensible to almost everyone else. It will be one of the most rigorous stages—emotionally, physically, and academically—you will pass through in your life. Not because you are expected to memorize every law, formula, and method with which you are inundated, but because you are being taught how to think analytically to become a professional problem solver (you'll hear this a lot).

Let's see, this is Chapter 4, so by now you should have a sense of what you are getting into or have already gotten into. But there is still more for you to learn! Engineering is an exclusive club. Attrition is high. Those who make it to graduation day to become engineers have talents and traits that got them there. These are inherent talents and traits, like problem solving (Before moving into your dorm room, did you mentally rearrange the furniture to maximize floor space?), resilience, determination, intelligence, and precision. You may meet a few lazy engineers, but you will never meet a dumb one.

THE TIME FRAME WE ARE LOOKING AT

How long does it take to get your bachelor's degree in engineering? *Too long* while wading through; *too short* once you've graduated. This is where the wizened older professor (looking over bifocals) would say: One's education *never* ends. Typically, once you have your high school diploma in hand, it takes four or five years[1] of full-time (usually nine months of the year) university schooling

---

[1]Should we get more specific? According to the National Society of Professional Engineers, the length of an engineering bachelor's degree is dependent on your path:

- 4 or 5 years at an accredited university.
- 2 years at a community college engineering transfer program and 2–3 years in a university engineering program.
- 3 years in a science or math major and 2 years in an engineering program.
- 5 or 6 years in an engineering co-op program.
- 8–10 years as an engineering evening student.

(The national average is close to 5 years.)

to complete the requirements for a bachelor's degree in an engineering discipline. The time frame may be shortened with summer school and AP credits.

Engineering course requirements are, in almost all cases, not open to any form of negotiation. So, once you decide to call the engineering buildings home, acquire two things: an advisor and a course catalog that spells out your degree requirements.

YOUR PROFESSORS

Engineering professors are an interesting bunch. It's hard to make any *real* generalizations about them that distinguishes them from professors in other departments. Yet, once you've had a few engineering classes, it's so obvious. They are just a bit well . . . *off.* They may laugh too loud or not at all, or they might wear polyester plaid pants with a striped shirt. More than one will be absent-minded. Some can intimidate with comments like, "My class has kept students out of medical school." Some are complacent and use the same yellowed notes they had 30 years ago. Many are hip, caring, and remember well what it was like to be in your shoes. Others are so enthusiastic about the material that you can't help but be, too.

While engineering professors seem like a distant race of enlightened individuals, they tend to be very human—at least most of the time! If you are frustrated with class material or scheduling, the best thing to do is to go talk with them.

Professors appreciate students who come to office hours—shows that you care! A few kindly souls have even been known to reschedule a test or due date if it falls on a day when you have two other tests.

Five Things You Will Hear a Professor Say
Sometime during Your Engineering Education

1. "Plug and chug" (Or "stick in the numbers and turn the crank").
2. "You kids probably don't even know what a slide ruler looks like."
3. "And now we will show a clip of the Tacoma Narrows Bridge collapse . . ."
4. "I took the exam myself and it only took a half hour. You guys will have three hours—it should be relatively straightforward."
5. "When I was your age, I had to run my programs with punch cards . . . and boy oh boy, if you got just one out of order and the cards weren't numbered . . . Wow!"

A Few Dos and Don'ts for Dealing with Profs

The goal is to be on the good side of every professor with whom you ever come in contact (and even those you don't). Whether you like them or not, they may be future references and colleagues.

- ☺ **Don't** be intimidated! You are missing out on great folks, help, and advice if you never talk to your professors.
- ☺ **Do** schedule appointments unless the professor has an open door policy.[2]
- ☺ **Don't** call professors at home: It's not the way to score points.
- ☺ **Do** go to office hours prepared. Have a list of questions ready. Think how frustrating it is in class when another student wastes everyone's time. Besides dealing with us, a professor very likely has at least another class, a handful of grad students, upcoming conferences, research projects, engineering association responsibilities, faculty issues, and funding proposals to take up his or her time.
- ☺ **Do** always address any difficulties (the textbook could be marketed as a sleeping aid) optimistically (you are learning some important terminology, but could the professor suggest a second reference? *Note:* Just be careful your professor isn't the author).

[2]An open door policy means you can come by the professor's office anytime.

☺ **Do** a quadruple check if you believe there has been a grading error on a test before you talk to the professor (see page 102). If you can, see the TA (teaching assistant) first. (A few professors have been known to dock additional points for students who complain unjustly about grading.)

ALL ABOUT ENGINEERS: CULTURE, CHARACTERISTICS, AND QUIRKS

We are a special breed (much beyond our traits and talents) that perhaps only we can fully appreciate.

The Great Divide: How to Tell Engineers from Nonengineers

What Gives Us Away	Engineers	Nonengineers
At the end of class	Watches start beeping	Rustle papers loudly and pack up their books
Calculators	Programmable, graphable, option of RPN and infrared interface	Standard checkbook style calculator (nothing more complicated than negative/ positive button)
ODEs	Ordinary differential equations	Poetry, but D and E shouldn't be capitalized like that. Did you run spell check?
e	~ 2.78	i before, except after c
When picking classes	Picking classes? Hopefully, no eight o'clocks this semester.	Can't be earlier than 10:00 A.M. and none on Friday.
Papers	huh?	Can pull out 10 pages in four hours (and still have time for spell check).
A "late night" is	Doing homework: 4:00 A.M. Going out: 1:00 A.M.	Writing a paper: 1:00 A.M. Going out: 4:00 A.M.

I know the answer! The answer lies within the heart of mankind! The answer is twelve? I think I'm in the wrong building.
—Marcie and Peppermint Patty of *Peanuts*

Programmable calculators with add-on capabilities; pocket protectors; crowded computer labs; mechanical pencils and green gridded paper; fabulous words like colloidal, thermodynamics, finite elements, eutectic, diodes, binary, gradients, flux, crystallography, eigenvectors; TAs' names you'll be lucky to pronounce, let alone remember; caffeine highs and sugar lows; lab or machine-shop goggles; camaraderie and unspoken understandings.

To say that the engineering experience is about what you learn would be akin to taking a blow-dryer to an iceberg. The experience is about the people you meet, the humor you are subjected to, and the environments in which you

live, work, and study. It really isn't so difficult to pinpoint a few differences that make us special (humbly so, of course).

- ☺ *Pride: Engineers know they are smart.* Of course. Rumor has it that scientific and programmable calculators are intentionally designed to look intimidating because we *like* that.

- ☺ *Stress level: Organized chaos.* There are only 24 hours in a day! So much material is covered in such a short time that it may seem disjointed and unconnected ("When will we ever use this?"). Somehow it all comes together and we manage to pull it off.

- ☺ *Humor: Quirky.* You will hear and even contribute a good share of bad jokes and puns. Hilarity will depend on your level of sleep deprivation.

- ☺ *Camaraderie: We will get through this together.* Because of our no-room-for-deviation course requirements, engineering students of the same discipline often have a majority of classes with the same group of people. This is especially true for the last two to three years when the classes are specific to the major or discipline. Mix this peer familiarity with the staggering workload and the result is a sense of unity from pulling together to learn from and help one another. Of course, not every school has the same workload, the same people, or even the same camaraderie, but at many places this proves true. It's hard not to bond with people with whom you have pulled many an all-nighter.

- ☺ *Competition: Exists.* Just how much or how little competition exists depends on your school. If you feel the chilly competitive edge of one or many of your classmates, you won't need to be told about it. There will always be one or two urchins who on the first day, check out every book in the library remotely related to the assigned project topic. The best thing for you to do is get the books first, then share. People who are out only for themselves get the reputation they deserve.

- ☺ *Fashion sense: Generally poor.* Especially when the safety goggles go to lunch with us.

- ☺ *Social stereotype: We don't attract many members of the opposite sex.* Well, engineers may not be known for their social skills (maybe the lack of), but they are notorious for playing as hard as they work.

☺ *The individual: You!* Most kids grow up wanting to be doctors, astronauts, or Michael Jordan—so why did we become engineers? There are supposedly two central influences that lead students to choose engineering: The first (boringly enough) is that we were good at math and science in high school; the second, we have a parent or other close relative working in a technical field. There are other theories about qualities, likes, and dislikes that we share, such as having a Sega or Nintendo somewhere in our personal histories, a perfectionist streak, and an appreciation for "tinkering."

> *I don't like writing papers.*
> *I like problem sets.*
> *I like building things.*
> *What's this fluffy design stuff?*
> —STANFORD UNIVERSITY
> MECHANICAL ENGINEERING
> SENIORS, Paraphrased
> commentary on their
> first design class

MORE ON INDIVIDUALS

The Female Engineer

Women have come a long way in the engineering profession, but on a linear scale, unfortunately, that still hasn't been very far. A visual survey of the faculty pictures on the engineering prof pic board reveals that female engineering professors are few in numbers and perhaps are even tokens.

As a female engineering student, the unfortunate reality is you will likely face some sort of discrimination during your college career. The problem is this: *Engineering is still an old boys' club.* When our folks were in school, engineering was seen as too technical, the machine shop too dirty, and the humor too crass for women. Because the professors now are mostly of our parents' generation (and older), the mind-set still exists, and women aren't always judged by their competence.

As ironic as it seems, the difficulty women face as engineering students *is* preparation for the difficult situations they will face as practicing engineers. When faced with an obnoxious comment or a disparaging remark, the best way women should handle the situation is with tact and dignity. Allow the offending speaker to see that you are above such behavior. If you are faced with a more serious situation of discrimination or harassment, contact the university women's center.

On the social side, a female engineer can have a lot of fun and can find being an engineer personally rewarding. Female students in engineering tend to strongly support each other and have a sense of sisterhood that other majors could never offer. Female engineers also tend to be acquainted with more of their classmates (male and female), and work better with diverse groups of people when working on projects or presentations. If you are a female

engineer, the guy-girl ratio may be working in your favor, but many women opt to date outside of engineering.

*Six Cool and Interesting Facts about Women Engineers**

1. Women engineering students tend to be more persistent than their male counterparts.
2. Female engineering students were found to be more active in their campus community than women in other majors, with involvement in honorary society leadership positions, sports teams, greek organizations, and community service groups.
3. When thinking about transferring out of engineering, women students are more likely to seek advice from a faculty member or upperclassman than women in other disciplines. (Sounds something like the male dislike of asking for directions, eh?)
4. Most women engineering students tended to like math better than the sciences in high school, while most male engineering students tended to like the sciences better than math.
5. Research found that women undergraduate engineering students have better academic credentials than the men. In 1975 (before affirmative action) 76 percent of women engineers reported they had a high school grade point average (GPA) greater than B+ while only 36 percent of men engineers claimed a GPA greater than B+. Even more striking was that almost 3 out of 10 (28.8 percent of) women had an A or A+ average in high school compared with 7 percent of men.
6. Freshmen women engineering students are younger than their male counterparts: 9 out of 10 are 18 years old or younger, while 3 out of 4 freshmen male engineers are 18 or younger. Women engineering students are also younger than nonengineering women.

A great resource for women in engineering is the Society of Women Engineers (SWE). Although underutilized, SWE is very active on most campuses and provides a forum for women to meet and interact with other women in engineering and industry. SWE chapters have social events such as ice-cream socials and pizza parties, and useful informational workshops for the entire (men and women) engineering community on everything from internship-finding to "evenings with industry" where practicing engineers from different companies and backgrounds are invited to speak.

A second resource, especially when looking for a job or internship, is *Diversity/Careers in Engineering & Information Technology*, a free magazine for woman, ethnic minorities, and people with disabilities. For more information, turn to page 34.

The Minority Engineer

Twenty years ago, 98 percent of practicing engineers in the United States were white males. Current statistics show that 40 percent of engineering grads are women, ethnic minorities, and foreign nationals. While it can be tough to glean

---

*See Ott and Reese entry in Bibliography for further information.

much solid information from these statistics, a glance into any engineering classroom will confirm recent trends. The problem is that we are waiting for those 20 years to catch up with the teaching staff. Women professors may be tokens, but African-American, Hispanic, and Native-American professors and instructors seem to be nonexistent. Hopefully their presence in the classroom is just a matter of time.

African-American engineering students who graduated from non-HBCUs (Historically Black Colleges and Universities) give vastly different reports of their college experiences, from having excellent peer interaction and heavy recruitment upon graduation, to having less than excellent experiences with standoffish classmates and difficult group project situations. Engineering students tend to form small groups to help each other cope with the workload and difficult concepts and assignments. These groups have mostly a social basis; for example, fraternities are well known to have extensive networks of information with past problem sets on file dating back 10 years. At many schools, there is an obvious lack of cohesion and information sharing between minority and nonminority students in engineering classes (and undoubtedly others). Minority students who cope best with this sort of situation are those who get on well socially and academically with both groups.

Six Things for the Minority Engineer to Tap Into

1. *Societies.* Minority engineering organizations like the Society of Hispanic Professional Engineers (SHPE), the American Indian Science and Engineering Society (AISES), and the National Society of Black Engineers (NSBE) are the strongest and best supported of *all* student engineering groups. These organizations and others listed in Appendix B provide an excellent network of support, mentors, and future job contacts.

2. *Diversity/Careers in Engineering & Information Technology magazine.*

   www.diversitycareers.com

   It's free and it's cool! This magazine is published twice yearly for all minorities (women, people with disabilities, and ethnic minorities). Although the target audience is juniors and seniors with articles on topics like starting the job hunt, it offers insight for any minority engineer. If you can't find the brightly covered magazine at a society meeting or your minority engineering program office, peruse their web sites. If you are looking for a job or internship, the web site also offers an on-line resume service.

3. *Scholarships and fellowships.*

   www.finaid.com (Click on the "Minority Students" link.)

   If you are worried about making ends meet, look up the National Association of Student Financial Aid Administrators (NASFAA) FinAid web site or head to the library and look for directories that list scholarships, fellowships, and financial aid for minority students.

4. *Major contributors to engineering and science.* Without much publicity, minority engineers have made remarkable contributions to research, development, invention, science, education, society, *and* engineering. Here are just a few of the groundbreakers and those who shattered the glass ceilings:

Sarah Boone (African-American inventor of the ironing board), Mario Molina (Hispanic researcher whose work on chlorofluorocarbons led to the phasing out of their use worldwide), Benjamin Banneker (African-American mathematician, astronomer, and member of the commission that planned Washington, D.C.), Wilfred Foster Denetclaw (Native-American researcher on development of skeletal muscle), Ellen Ochoa (Hispanic astronaut), Garrett Augustus Morgan (African-American inventor of the gas mask and automatic street light), W. B. Purvis (African-American inventor of the fountain pen), Narciso Monturiol (Hispanic pioneer in underwater navigation who drove the first fully operable submarine).

5. *The future.* They've been there, done it, and made it. Minorities in industry and research are extremely supportive of you in your endeavors whether looking for a job, internship, or simply advice. Look them up.

6. *Those behind you.* Although, the number of minority students in engineering programs has increased dramatically in the past decade, the overall numbers are still fairly low.[3] What can you do? Get high profile on campus with leadership positions! Get involved off campus in recruitment programs and outreach programs to get those numbers up!

The "Older" (Returning to School) Engineer

What makes a student "older"? Maturity level. Younger students see reentry students as the folks who ask good questions in class and really do understand things on the first pass. Reentry students are those who had a previous full-time career or job, have children/spouses, or any combination of the above. One's route to engineering can take many paths.

Students returning from other life activities to become engineers tend to have a stronger sense of mission and determination because they are making more compromises and sacrifices than the average student fresh out of high school. Professors recognize this and treat returning students with added respect, *not* because they don't respect the younger students but because, on the whole, older students are more motivated to learn and pay closer attention. Not surprisingly, they also get better grades.

Returning engineering students will not find the same flexibility in classes that other returning students may find. Balancing school and study with work and family commitments takes ingenuity and compromise. Often you can take the introductory classes in Math, Physics, Biology, Computer Science, and Chemistry after work at a junior or community college. After the intros, however, most necessary classes are offered only during the day and your engineering classes will become a full-time endeavor.

If you are returning to school to become an engineer or even just thinking about it, you will have many of the same concerns and issues as any other student, plus a few more.

---

[3]The National Science Foundation reported that in the early 1990s the number of African Americans, Hispanics, and Native Americans increased in engineering programs 44 percent, 47 percent, and 58 percent, respectively. But in 1996 African Americans earned only 7 percent of total degrees, Hispanics earned 5 percent, and Native Americans earned 0.5 percent.

☺ *Time for review.* If it's been awhile since you've had Trig, Geometry, or Calculus, it is usually necessary to jump back and retake or audit[4] the last math class you took or check out a study guide that can refresh your memory. The same may be true for the foundation science classes.

☺ *"Yikes—this is so hard."* In the beginning, many returning engineering students feel behind their younger peers and overwhelmed by the amount of work, material covered, and unfamiliar concepts they are expected to digest at what seems lightning speed. Not to worry! By the end of your first year back, you will most likely be ahead of your classmates.

☺ *Most bosses are supportive of returning students.* Don't be afraid to approach them about readjusting work hours, shifts, or workloads.

☺ *Check out the Center for Adult Students.* Many campuses have a center or organization for reentry students that offers workshops, lunchtime seminars, and a network to meet others who are doing the same juggling act you are.

☺ *You will become a different person after returning to school.* You will make new friends and meet many new people; you will also have new ideas, goals, and interests. This can be alarming to someone close to you who is not in school because he or she may feel that they are unable to grow with you. Include spouses at school social functions, take them to a favorite class (this is done all the time), and take time to show them what you are learning.

☺ *The married re-entry student's life.* Married students who return to school may have additional issues to face, including how to support a spouse or have a spouse support them.

1. **Work out a plan *and* a backup plan with your spouse.**

    Engineering is more intensive than any other program you could choose and that may be more difficult for them to understand. Working things out to a manageable level for everyone will take compromise and support from family members and/or partner.

2. **If you have children, don't be afraid to ask for and accept help.**

    A single or married parent who returns to school is able to do so more successfully with the assistance of grandparents, employers, church congregations, and day cares.

3. **More than any other student, get organized!**

    You are the person for whom organizers were created. Write down everything (EVERYTHING!) you can possibly remember that takes time, even dinner or going to church on Sunday.

---

[4]*Auditing* a class means you go to the class primarily to listen to the lecture. You might do the homework on your own, but you do not typically receive feedback from the instructor or official credit for the course. Schools and even professors will differ their policies for auditing a course. Some professors request that you participate in the class like a regular student, while other professors are pleased to simply have a motivated individual who enjoys their lectures. The great thing about auditing is that it often is free or inexpensive.

4. Female returning students feel a higher level of stress and guilt.

This guilt stems from their not being as available as they would like to their families or partner. If you recognize yourself here, understand that your being in school will be better for everyone in the end.

CHAPTER 5

Choosing a Major and Selecting Classes

The school should always have as its aim that the young man leave it as a harmonious personality, not as a specialist. This in my opinion is true in a certain sense even for technical schools . . . The development of general ability for independent thinking and judgment should always be placed foremost, not the acquisition of special knowledge.
—ALBERT EINSTEIN, German-American Physicist (1879–1955)

CHOOSING A MAJOR

Every major will tell you that their discipline is the best. So undoubtedly will the department chair at the departmental overview. Professors and "let's explore engineering" books divide the disciplines or majors into three groups: classical engineering (an early Egyptian had the same major), modern engineering (Thomas Edison invented your major), and specialty engineering (there aren't very many of you with the same major). However, you really need to be concerned with only two groups that are important in reaching your long-term engineering goals: Mainstream disciplines and Narrower-focused disciplines.

Mainstream disciplines are those that most universities with schools of engineering offer, majors like Civil Engineering, Mechanical Engineering, Electrical Engineering, Industrial Engineering, Chemical Engineering, and Computer Science (which we'll consider engineering). These Mainstream majors are broader in subject range and have a better selection of technical and engineering electives.

Narrower-focused engineering disciplines are tailored around and concentrate on a specific engineering field by combining knowledge from different Mainstream disciplines. These Narrower disciplines are often considered a branch of the Mainstream majors and include fields such as Geophysical Engineering, Ocean Engineering, Forestry Engineering, Construction Engineering, and Welding Engineering. The best way to learn more about the different engineering disciplines is to check out school department and society web sites (See Appendix A) or talk to professional engineers.

If you aren't in college yet (or even if you are), another great source of information on the different engineering disciplines and engineering in general is JETS (Junior Engineering Technical Society). JETS provides reference materials on engineering to high school students, teachers, and counselors in addition to sponsoring programs and design competitions that allow students to "try on" engineering. See the society listings in Appendix B for JETS' E-mail and phone number.

Mainstream and Narrower-focused disciplines are the two end points on the spectrum of possible majors, not simply headings under which every offered engineering major must be listed. It is recommended that if you are not *absolutely* certain about the best preparation for a profession in a discipline you are *absolutely* certain you will *absolutely and utterly* love then you should pick a major that is not Narrower-focused. However, if you are excited by your potential narrow major—go for it.

Here's a quick quiz that might help straighten things out if you think you might want to choose a more Narrowly-focused degree:

	Yes	No
1. Did you choose your school because it offered a specific major?	☐	☐
2. Are you returning to school after more than one year off?	☐	☐
3. Do you consider yourself an active person with many interests?	☐	☐
4. Did you have difficulty deciding on a major?	☐	☐

Spectrum of Engineering Majors

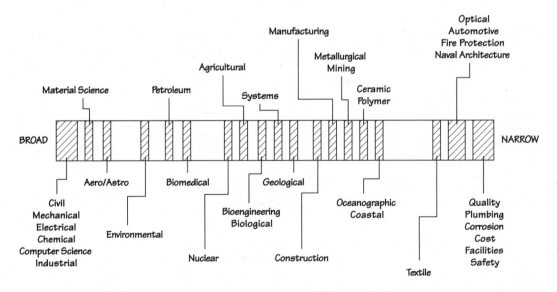

5. Have you spoken with practicing engineers about their profession?   ☐   ☐

6. Do you know who Mary Anderson is?   ☐   ☐

Points: 1. yes—1, no—0; 2. yes—1, no—0; 3. yes—0, no—1; 4. yes—0, no—1; 5. yes—1, no—0; 6. yes—liar, no—the inventor of the windshield wiper and a well known hydrogeologist.

So what does this all mean? Nothing, really, if you are already choosing a Mainstream major, but if are thinking about choosing a Narrower-focused major then you should consider your quiz results. The closer your points are to the maximum of five, the more confident you should feel about choosing a Narrower-focused major. If you think Construction Engineering sounds cool but you scored a two on the quiz, then take some electives in the department and look into pairing a construction minor with a more versatile degree in Civil Engineering.

Once you have started taking engineering classes, changing your major could be costly in terms of your time and money. Credits don't transfer easily the way they do for your friends in arts and sciences. So keep several things in mind when making a final decision about your major:

☺ *A good time to specialize in a field is during graduate school.* Companies that hire for a specialized area usually hire folks with graduate work in that specific field.

☺ *Professional Engineering (P.E.) certification exams are offered only in certain disciplines.* Civil, Electrical, Mechanical, Chemical, Environmental, Structural, Agricultural, Control Systems, Fire Protection, Industrial, Manufacturing, Metallurgical, Mining/Mineral, Nuclear, and Petroleum. If you hope some day to consult in private practice or have the authority to sign off on documents and work submitted to the government, you must be a PE certified engineer. To learn more about becoming a PE, turn to page 133 in Chapter 11.

☺ *The more mainstream your degree, the more versatile you are in the job market.* Also, you are less at the mercy of specific technical economies and markets.

☺ *Trust your instinct based on your life experience.*

☺ *Galileo changed his major.*

MINORS, DOUBLE MAJORS, HONORS DEGREES, AND OTHER THINGS

An added distinction to your degree is always nice. It offers you more flexibility in your job search and offers employers a more versatile potential employee. Check if there are special programs or minors available at your university for engineering students. Some curricula in one discipline include so many classes from another that a minor or honors distinction may be only an extra two or three classes away. Discuss your options with your advisor.

SELECTING AND REGISTERING FOR CLASSES, SORT OF

Except for electives, engineers aren't so much able to select classes as they are able to select *sections*[1] of classes. Upon notifying the university that you will be attending their esteemed institution, you are likely to receive a handbook with a course schedule similar in detail to the one given on the next page (err . . . especially if you chose ME).

Hmm . . . not a whole lot of room for flipping through the course catalog and selecting random classes that sound interesting. What can you do to make a rigid schedule less constraining? Here are 10 tips to make your schedule and time work for you.

1. Don't overburden yourself the first semester of your freshman year.
Just as you didn't learn to ride a bike overnight without training wheels and a few scrapes, so you need to ease into college life and its academic demands. Allow yourself a lighter load first semester and expect some bruises. How well you do your first semester very often sets the tone for your remaining semesters.

---

[1]A section is a subdivision of a course. For a class like Introduction to Chemistry, there might be 300 fellow students in your lecture, but only 15 in your lab *section*. In Calc I or II there may be 300 students taking the course, but you would only see the 15–20 in your section. Different sections are usually offered at different times, and sometimes have different professors.

Specimen Curriculum for Mechanical Engineering

FRESHMEN YEAR		Semester Hours	
		Fall	Spring
Chem 102a,b	General Chemistry (I & II)	4	4
Math 172a,b	Analytic Geometry & Calculus (I & II)	4	4
	Elective		3
ES 130	Engineering Science Modeling and Simulation	3	
Physics 117a	Elementary Physics I		4
CS 101 or 102	Programming and Problem Solving		3
	Total	14	15

Note: Materials Science 151 (Introduction to Materials Science) is a 4-hour course that may be substituted for Chemistry 102b.

SOPHOMORE YEAR		Semester Hours	
		Fall	Spring
Math 222	Analytic Geometry and Calculus (III)	3	
Physics 117b	Elementary Physics (II)	4	
ME 160	Mechanical Engineering Modeling	3	
CE 180	Statics	3	
	Elective	3	3
Math 229	Elementary Differential Equations		3
ME 190	Dynamics		3
EE 112	Electrical Engineering Science		3
ME 171	Instrumentation Laboratory		2
ME 220a	Thermodynamics I		3
	Total	16	17

JUNIOR YEAR		Semester Hours	
		Fall	Spring
ME 200	Kinematics	3	
ME 212	Engineering Mechanics Laboratory	2	
ME 213	Energetics Laboratory		2
ME 220b	Thermodynamics II	3	
CE 182	Mechanics of Materials	3	
ME 201	Design of Machine Elements		3
ME 244	Fluid Dynamics	3	
	Elective	6	9
	Total	17	17

Note: ME 212 and ME 213 may be taken in either order.

SENIOR YEAR		Semester Hours	
		Fall	Spring
ME 202	Design Synthesis	3	
ME 263	Heat Transfer	3	
ME 257	Engineering Systems Analysis		3
ME 203	Senior Design Projects		3
	Electives	9	9
	Total	15	15

Elective Breakdown and Requirements: Social Sciences Electives = 9 hours and Humanities Electives = 6 hours (at least 3 hours in each must be at 200-level), Math (above 229) = 3 hours, Technical Electives = 9 hours, Technology and Society Electives = 6 hours, and Open Electives = 6 hours.

You will learn your limits by pushing them—and others' expectations of you by sometimes not meeting them. A strong academic first semester lays a solid foundation on which to build your remaining college years; a less-than-strong first semester can dig you a hole from which you must climb out before you start on the foundation.

2. Check out the professor before you register for his or her section.

A professor who bounces around the classroom on a pogo stick to demonstrate kinetic and potential energy will not only keep you awake and entertain you, but engrave the concept and application in your mind. Your like or dislike of a professor and his or her teaching methods makes a huge difference in your interest and success in that class, your enthusiasm for the subject, and even your confidence in choosing engineering as a career. Upperclassmen are an excellent source of information when selecting classes.

Is Your Professor Live . . . or Televised?

Some pros and cons to taking the televised class at home

Pros	Cons
✔ Professor is often an excellent lecturer.	✘ Paying attention can be tough.
✔ Convenient.	✘ Easy to tape and never watch.
✔ Classes can be taped and watched a second time.	✘ Feeling of detachment; may be intimidating to search out TA.
	✘ No interaction during lecture—questions have to wait.

> ☞ A famous or accomplished professor isn't always the best educator. Ask around about his or her teaching style and availability to students.

3. Take classes in the recommended sequence.

This seems fairly obvious, but . . . A lot of schedules are ideally arranged so that concepts taught in one class will carry over into other classes taught at the same time. For example, from our sample curriculum schedule (see previous page), you can test the concepts from CE 182 Mechanics of Materials first semester junior year in the ME 212 Engineering Mechanics Laboratory experiments. Although the course guide states that labs ME 212 and 213 do not have to be taken in a specific order, you should take classes so they complement each other. It will be much less work for you.

4. Be realistic—don't take an eight o'clock if you won't get up.

For some people getting up for an eight o'clock class is no problem, but lectures at two o'clock on Friday afternoons (especially when ski season arrives) are another story.

5. Fill course requirements early.

Get them out of the way! If you think taking *another* math class again next semester is torture, try taking it second semester senior year when you can't remember *anything*. Are depth, breadth, and technical electives being met with the courses you have selected? Double-check with your advisor. A mistake could force you to attend summer school.

6. Don't schedule more than three classes back to back in one day.

Active listening and critical thinking can be taxing on the ol' noggin, so give yourself a break by breaking up your schedule. Otherwise, you may find yourself paying more attention to the school newspaper crossword puzzle than your ardent professor.

7. Be wise in choosing nonengineering electives.

These are the classes that fill the Renaissance-student requirements needed for your diploma. They can provide some much-needed stimulation for the left side of the brain, but recognize that engineers already carry a heavy workload. Thus, you should be careful what you choose or you'll find yourself struggling with time and frustration.

Having trouble deciding between two electives? Visit the bookstore and browse through the textbooks for the classes you are considering.

Some Considerations for Choosing Nonengineering Electives

BEWARE of classes that. . .	CHOOSE classes that. . .
✘ May be too reading intensive (literature survey classes).	✔ Are discussion oriented.
✘ May be research intensive (like Readings in Old Norse and you don't speak or read Old Norse).	✔ Are recommended by other engineers.
✘ Have substantial added fieldwork, language labs or films outside of class time.	✔ Are unique to your university or are taught by famous professors.
✘ You aren't enthusiastic about.	✔ You've always been intrigued by.
✘ Have prerequisites.	✔ Are a change of pace from your required classes for the term.
	✔ Improve your communication skills for a future job.

Does this mean you shouldn't take a random class that looks interesting because it will demand a bit more time? Definitely not, but evaluate how the workload from it will fit in with your engineering workload, extracurricular commitments, and social schedule. Although it would be fun to take an elective in scuba or Web design, you'd probably get more out of the course if you took it during the summer when more time is available.

> ⚠ **Ahem, one last thing** . . . You also might want to avoid taking any classes that you don't want future references, employers, or graduate schools to see on your transcript (e.g., Modern Sexuality and Eroticism). Of course, you can always opt to sit in on the course.

Who Decides What Engineering Students Learn?

While your university may determine how to best present an engineering education to you, ABET (Accreditation Board for Engineering and Technology) is the national organization that officially determines whether your university's engineering programs measure up to the engineering profession's standards. To accredit a program, a team of practicing engineers reviews the qualifications of the faculty, the adequacy of teaching facilities (including laboratories, equipment, computer resources, and libraries), and the work done by the students. Each university program must meet or exceed the minimum requirements established by the profession to receive certification.

By 2001 a new and hopefully improved set of criteria (Criteria 2000) will be used for evaluation. Graduates of accredited programs must be able to meet measurable standards not only in technical proficiency but also in communication skills and knowledge of engineering in a greater social and global context. In some states, to be eligible for a professional engineering license (for more info see page 133), you must have graduated from an ABET-accredited program.

8. Look into taking nonengineering pass/fails.

It's the best of both worlds: getting credit for a class without having to do a lot of work. Pass/fail (sometimes also called credit/no-credit or credit/no clue) policies vary from university to university and even from department to department, so check with your advisor to see if pass/fail is an option.

9. Register as early as possible for classes.

Putting off registering or forgetting to do so until later can strand you in a Monday evening Chem lab that directly conflicts with prime-time football. Registering early also gives you a better chance of getting a better professor— open classes and sections with good professors offered in late morning and early afternoon slots fill up quickly. Also note cutoff dates to drop, withdraw, and add a course.

10. After freshman year, lighten your second semester or spring quarter loads.

A lighter load does not necessarily mean taking fewer hours, but perhaps lightening up other commitments; for example, cutting down on extracurricular involvement or part-time job hours (if financially possible). Christmas vacation and spring break are usually not enough to recharge most students' internal batteries. The way to fight fatigue is to plan for it. See tips on fighting burnout in Chapter 9.

One more thing to think about when choosing classes. The two-part Fundamentals of Engineering (FE) exam is the first step in becoming a certified professional engineer (refer to Chapter 11 for more information). The FE (also called the EIT or Engineer in Training) tests engineering students in the following areas:

- *Mathematics.* Differential and integral calculus and differential equations, probability and statistics, linear algebra, numerical analysis and advanced calculus may be included.
- *Science.* General chemistry and general physics, life science, earth science, advanced chemistry and advanced physics may be included.
- *Engineering science.* Creative applications of science and mathematics, mechanics (fluid mechanics, dynamics, statics, etc.), electrical and electronic circuits, material science, thermodynamics, and computers.
- *Nontechnical areas.* Engineering economics and ethics.

If you have an extra technical elective to fill and haven't taken a class in one of these subjects, increase your versatility in engineering and preparedness for the FE exam by taking one of them.

CHAPTER 6

In Class—More to Staying Awake than Taking Notes?

It can take until junior year before you really feel like an engineer in your selected discipline. Your freshman and sophomore years are spent getting the background, the skills, and the tools that you will need for your major: math to understand the proofs and derivations, computer skills to set up both analytical and illustrative models, and confidence in your own best methods of analysis and problem solving. Engineering, as you will read in this book and hear many times at school, builds on itself. All that math you take during the first years of college is *frequently* used later on, not only in the sophomore, junior, and senior years, but also in summer internships, graduate school, and your life as an engineer. Notes from a freshmen computer science programming lab may be hauled out and dusted off to find the command to solve your senior year design project.

Unlike our arts and humanities counterparts, we do need to absorb as much as we can from *every* class to ensure a strong basis for the next level of learning. During a particularly hard week, sitting still in a marginally comfortable desk for more than 10 minutes might fool your brain into thinking it's time for sleep (yippee!). Your manipulation of the classroom environment and your preparedness for the course offer the most buoyancy in these tidal wave times. In this section strategic ideas are offered on note-taking, paying attention, getting more out of classes and laboratory periods, and recognizing the important elements of a course that will assist you in conserving time and energy and establishing some good(!) habits early on.

THE CLASSROOM ENVIRONMENT

One of your classrooms might be a small stuffy room with a noisy heater at the end of the hall; another might be a huge lecture hall with hard, tiny seats and constricting desktops. The psych major will inform you of the salutary wall and ceiling colors of the psychology building and transcontinental McDonalds, but unfortunately *that* train of thought was derailed before pulling into the

engineering buildings. OK, so there may not be a whole lot you can do about your classroom to encourage paying attention to the professor, but you *can* control where you sit. Keep these things in mind before grabbing the seat closest to the door.

☺ *Sit smart.* Believe it or not, studies have shown that the closer a student sits to the front of the class, the better that student does in the course. The details are sketchy, and it seems a tad odd that someone would research this subject, but take it for what it's worth. The best advice is sit near the door if you are late (so you won't disrupt the class), in the back if you want to nap or do other homework, and otherwise wherever you are comfortable.

☺ *Is your professor a leftie?* For classes in which you copy a lot of notes from the chalkboard, sit on the left side of the classroom if your professor is left-handed and on the right side of the class if your professor is right-handed. This helps with professors who seem to write faster than 3×10^8 *m/s* (speed of light), but perpetually eclipse the chalkboard.

☺ *Call it seat security.* The seat an engineering student sits in the first day of the semester or quarter is often the one to which he or she returns each time that class meets. If it isn't the same seat, it is often in the same area of the classroom. Comfort through familiarity? Students in most other academic schools don't share our peculiarity; obviously they haven't considered the convenience of sitting next to a side wall chalkboard (chalk-holder = caffeinated drink-holder). Why is this glimpse into the engineering psyche interesting to know? Save someone from bewildering displacement later on by grabbing a good seat the first day of class.

NOTE TAKING AND PAYING ATTENTION

Not only are they related, but *note taking and paying attention are entwined.* Taking good notes may get you good grades even if you never look at them. How? Because to take good notes, you must listen actively to your professor. Active listening means digesting the information and making the connection between the theories and the applicable examples. Of course, you should frequently look over notes from your classes, but even then, isn't it much nicer to go over complete, neat, informative notes that are properly organized in chronological order? So for EXCELLENT notes that lead to MOST EXCELLENT grades:

1. Listen actively!

For the reasons explained above. A few hints for maintaining alertness at times of trouble.

Want to Stay Awake? Try this . . .

First Period
(the 7:00 or 8:00 A.M. class)

☺ Eat a healthy breakfast (A cereal called Sugar Bombs may sugar bomb you in the middle of class).

☺ Get up and do something nonsedentary before class—go for a quick jog, run an errand.

☻ Could you secretly be a morning person? Try going to bed and getting up to study *before* class.

The Drowsy after-Lunch Period
(1:00 or 2:00 P.M. classes)

☻ Eat lunch after class or somehow readjust your meals so that postmeal drowsiness doesn't set in while you are in class.
☻ Sleep in, go to class alert.

Tuesday and Thursday Periods
(Or any other unusually long class)

☻ Save and use your nice pens so note-taking is kind of fun.
☻ Don't sit anywhere near friends or someone you will want to distract or talk with.
☻ Be prepared for class. You'll find it becomes much more interesting.

Last Class of the Day Period

☻ Almost there! Just get through this period.
☻ Bribe yourself.
☻ Remind yourself that you want to learn this only once.

2. Use binders and keep a hole-punch in your backpack.

Halfway through the semester those spiral notebooks get bent, the pages won't turn, and those notes you xeroxed a couple of weeks ago have vanished. Some people just aren't binder people, but engineers should be—it's so logical. Class handouts can be immediately integrated with notes (thus the hole-punch) and binders allow for note rearrangement for studying convenience.

> **Binders** can be divided to include more than one subject (the Monday-Wednesday-Friday binder) or all your subjects to cut down on the weight in your backpack and the probability that a book is forgotten at home.

3. Date everything, including handouts.

Most people do it anyway. It makes things so much easier at exam time and when discussing class or a problem with your classmates over the phone ("But look in your notes and see what he said on January 26 about thermoplastics").

4. Copy everything the professor writes down or reiterates.

Engineering professors are not usually discussion oriented. So if they write something on the chalkboard, it is probably important for you to comprehend or at least refer back to later for help with problem sets. If the notes on the chalkboard are nearly verbatim to the course textbook, still copy them down. Copying and listening will keep you focused now, thus saving time reviewing the text later. What about the professor who forgets about the chalkboard until he illustrates a picture from a "really good" engineering anecdote?—make note of what topics he hits and study the text.

5. Leave gaps on the page, not in your notes.

Pages that are broken up with bullets, headings, and diagrams are much more fun to read (easier anyway) than pages of compressed writing. Is there a paper shortage? Leaving spaces on the notepaper also allows for later study additions or relevant notes (see number 6).

6. Use two colors of ink.

A nifty idea is to use one color for what the professor writes on the chalkboard and a second color for your own supplements to the professor's notes. The supplements can be clarifying comments or examples the professor mentions, definitions in the text, or even questions to ask during office hours. The benefits of using the two colors is to be able to distinguish what the professor deems important from your supplementary information.

☞ **Use inks that won't run or bleed.** If getting caught in a downpour isn't bad enough, losing good notes will worsen your mood considerably. Waterproof ink (ballpoints and some felt tips) also allows for highlighting without bleeding.

---

7. Box, underline, or highlight important equations, useful definitions, and theories.

All the equations begin to run together when there's a proof involved or even when "simplifying" another equation. If your professor deems anything important: box it, star it, highlight it. Somehow make it jump out at you from the rest of your notes because it will appear later on a test. Guaranteed.

8. Employ a user-defined (your own) shorthand.

It saves time. And engineering professors often write so much that sometimes they recycle their own written-out notes from year to year on the overhead projectors. Your brand of shorthand also will keep your hand from cramping and save your brain from tedium. Use apostrophes! Use abbreviations! As long as you can understand it—use it. See the next page for some suggestions and examples.

9. Title examples.

Yes, it sounds rather odd. However, if a professor takes the time to go over an example, usually this problem illustrates something important. Chances are this "something important" will appear later in a problem set, a test, or an exam. Determine what makes each problem unique from the others discussed in the lecture. Classifying each example with a summarizing and distinguishing name helps the mind neatly file the method away and easily recognize a similar problem at test time. How would you title the following fluids problem?

Math Stuff:

Δ	change	#	number
(+)	positive	∞	infinity
(−)	negative	//	is parallel to
=	is equal to	$\perp$	is perpendicular to
$\neq$	is not equal to	i.e.	that is
$\equiv$	is defined by	e.g.	for example
$\cong$	is approximately equal to	cw or $\curvearrowright$	clockwise
$\sim$	approximately	ccw or $\curvearrowleft$	counterclockwise
$\overset{?}{=}$	might be equal to	✌	peace
$\rightarrow$	leads to	DEF	definition
$\uparrow$	increases	$\sphericalangle$	angle
$\downarrow$	decreases	<	section
$\Sigma(..)$	sum of (...)	$\Pi(..)$	product of

Taking-Notes Stuff

FS	factor of safety	abs.	absolute
impt.	important	cont.	continued
rel.	relative	b/c or ∵	because
w/	with	w/o	without
∴	therefore	eqn.	equation
mat'l.	material	sol'n.	solution
		hmk	homework

Q.E.D. Quod Erat Demonstrandum—which was to be demonstrated, used at the end of math proofs.

An Excerpt from Some Lecture Somewhere . . .

Your Fluids professor says:

"OK—to illustrate flow over a flat plate normal to the flow, let's consider the force on a billboard exerted by an 80 mph wind during a hurricane. Remember that wall shear stress won't contribute to the drag force in this situation. The billboard is 30 feet by 10 feet with a thickness of 1 foot. The wind is blowing normal to it. We'll assume the kinematic viscosity and density of air to be 1.8×10^{-4} ft²/s and 0.00237 slug/ft³, respectively." (She is drawing on the billboard as she talks.)

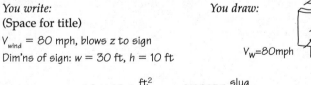

You write:
(Space for title)
V_{wind} = 80 mph, blows z to sign
Dim'ns of sign: w = 30 ft, h = 10 ft

You draw:

$$\underline{\text{ASSUMPTIONS}}: \ v = 1.8 \times 10\text{-}4 \ \frac{ft^2}{s}, \rho = 0.00237 \ \frac{slug}{ft^3}$$

Fluids Professor:

"Converting the wind velocity to feet per second, we have 117 ft/s. Now calculating the Reynold's number with the sign *width* we get 6.50×10^6." (Also writing the equation on the board). So what does our Reynold's number tell us?

You add:

$$Re = \frac{Vw}{v} = \frac{(117\ ft/s)(30\ ft)}{(1.8 \times 10\text{-}4\ ft^2/s)} = 1.95 \times 107$$ USE WIDTH

Fluids Professor:

"So what does our Reynold's number tell us? We'll use Figure 9.10 on page 442 because our Reynold's number is greater than one thousand. To use the chart we need a b-to-h ratio, so for us that is billboard width to billboard thickness which is equal to 30. Reading off the chart we maybe have a drag coefficient of perhaps 1.6."

You add:

$Re \geq 10^3$—use FIGURE 9.10 on page 442.

$$\frac{b}{h} = \frac{w}{t} = \frac{30\ ft}{1\ ft} = 30 \quad \rightarrow \quad \text{Chart gives } C_D \approx 1.6$$

Fluids Professor:

"And finally now we can use our Drag Equation getting. Plugging and chugging, our correct answer is 7786 pounds."

Your notes:
(Space for title)
$V_{wind} = 80$ mph, blows $\perp$ to sign
Dim'ns of sign: w = 30 ft, h = 10 ft

ASSUMPTIONS: $v = 1.8 \times 10\text{-}4\ \frac{ft^2}{s}$, $\rho = 0.00237\ \frac{slug}{ft^3}$

$$Re = \frac{Vw}{v} = \frac{(117\ ft/s)(30\ ft)}{(1.8 \times 10\text{-}4\ ft^2/s)} = 1.95 \times 10^7$$ USE WIDTH

$Re \geq 10^3 \rightarrow$ use FIGURE 9.10 on page 442.

$$\frac{b}{h} = \frac{w}{t} = \frac{30\ ft}{1\ ft} = 30 \quad \rightarrow \quad \text{Chart gives } C_D \approx 1.6$$

$$D = \frac{1}{2}C_D\rho V^2 A \quad \underline{\text{Drag eqn.}}$$

$$D = \frac{1}{2}(1.6)\left(0.00237\ \frac{slug}{ft^3}\right)\left(117\ \frac{ft}{s}\right)^2 [(30\ ft)(10\ ft)]$$

$$= 7786\ lbf$$

After copying this down, how would you characterize this problem? What's important in this example? What equations do you use? What distinguishes this problem from other problems?

Some good titles might be:

- Wind Drag on Sign
- Sign problem
- Drag on flat plate normal to flow
- Gone with the wind

⚠ **A Note on . . . NOTES.** Save everything. No cooking s'mores or weinies over engineering notes, you'll *need* and *use* them again.

This section might more lamely be called "How to Get Your Tuition's Worth" or "How to Maximize Your In-Class Learning and Understanding." Here are a few things to consider that will help you cut some corners on the map of time (and exam-time cramming).

1. Bring what you need to class.

☺ *Yourself!* Let's apply some of our analytical engineering thinking to demonstrate the importance of good class attendance (see *Three Choices: Choose Your Own Adventure* on the following page):

Notice from this example that it would still be better to go to class even if you might not pay attention (you will have a brainache some days) than it would be to skip class completely.

What else should you bring? That depends on the class and the professor.

☺ *Textbook.* Some professors will frequently refer to tables, charts, and examples in the textbook. So bring your textbook and note important topics and problems.

☺ *Straightedge, compass, graph paper, etc.* Bring any tools that will assist or speed up your neat note-taking; a university bookstore mini stencil speeds up drawing flowcharts or molecular configurations. A ruler (or student ID) makes for nicer graphs and diagrams.

☺ *Ministapler.* It's handy to have with you when problem sets are due every day or every other day. Having a stapler also makes you popular with your classmates.

☺ *Hole-punch.* Leave the industrial-size punch at home; a handheld one is sufficient. See page 51.

2. Avoid chatty classmates and entrancing posters.

That's interesting . . . [strain to read the poster] 3-D COMPUTER-AIDED MAPPING OF THE ADIRONDACKS. Nifty! . . . I wonder if my wilderness brochure came today. Hmm, gosh, I wonder if I got *any* mail today? Uh-oh, forgot to mail my credit card payment again.

Avoid anything that distracts or interferes with focusing your six senses on the professor's lecture. A conversation behind you can make it difficult to hear important questions. If you love the smell of tar, avoid the window seats until the parking lot is resurfaced.

3. Be prepared.

Being prepared for class by skimming recommended readings, reading (yes, actually reading) required readings, and working suggested problems cuts down on anxiety and on the amount of time you spend preparing for a test or exam. Going to class with a basic understanding of a concept allows you to ask questions in or right after class, instead of having to go to a professor's office hours or hunt down the TA. Additionally, the class will be more interesting if you understand the material before coming in because you are spending less

Go to Class— Tired, but Alert	Go to Class—Zzzz (You had a Biology test first period)	Skip Class (You go back to bed after first period)
Skim over recommended reading. = *20 min.* Grab a highly caffeinated soda or coffee after the first period test. Go to class, pay attention, take good notes, and understand class examples. = *50 min.* Look over notes later and read excerpts of recommended reading that are important. = *40 min.*	Go to class and snooze through about half of it. Notes are so-so. = *50 min.* Read all of recommended text to fill in holes in notes—What was important? = *1 hr., 45 min.* Unsure why height is used instead of width in class example. = *no time, just annoying* Call classmate to find out why width is used instead of height. (Hey, does anyone have a student directory I can borrow? Wait, what's her last name?) = *15 minutes*	Zzzz at home in bed. = *wasted tuition* Track someone down to get notes. = *10 min.* Go get notes. = *15 min.* Xerox notes and wait in line to pay. = *20 min.* Return notes. = *15 min.* Read over notes twice, but have difficulty deciphering handwriting. = *55 min. + frustration* Read all of recommended text. I *think* this section is supposed to be important. = *1 hr., 30 min.* In passing, learn from a friend that a different section is important. = *added frustration* Read again and comprehend the important section. Work the text example problems. = *1 hr.* Phone friend to ask why width is used instead of height in class example. Chat. = *15 min.*
= *1 hr., 50 min.*	= *2 hrs., 50 min.*	= *4 hrs., 30 min.* + *tuition wasted* + *frustration*

time digesting the information and comparing it to your own knowledge. The second time through the information, you are more apt to *listen* to what the professor is saying and the context in which it is being presented. The material has to be read/studied/looked over *sometime*, so just do it before class and save your time for merrier activities.

4. If you are *still* unclear about something, talk to the professor after class.

Class time isn't always the best time for a personal Q&A opportunity with a professor. Discuss the subject after class. If you have another class or your professor seems to be in a hurry, make an appointment before leaving. Ask questions as they occur so you aren't playing catch-up later.

SAVE THAT SYLLABUS

syl·la·bus, sil'*a*·bus, n. pl. **syl·la·bus·es, syl·la·bi,** syl'*la*·bi" An outline or other brief statement of the main points of a discourse, the subjects of a course of lectures, the contents of the curriculum.

Webster's College Dictionary, 1991

The first day of a class can be fun. It's a chance to find out who's in your class, speculate about how interesting the material and professor will be, and flip through a new textbook with a great title that intimidates your nonengineering roommates. The handing out of the syllabus signifies the end of vacation and the start of an intrguing new flood of information.

The syllabus also offers the rules of the road for a class and assistance in prioritizing your list of homework to do and subjects to study. Can I drop my lowest test score in this class? Are any tests open note or do I need to spend time memorizing the equations? How do the help sessions, office hours, tests, and problem sets in this class fit in with my other classes' help sessions, office hours, tests, and problem sets *and* my recreation schedule? Look over the syllabus on the next page and pick out what you think is important and note why. Exactly how you will juggle your other classes and activities while understanding this course's material can be hidden in the syllabus. Mark up the first CE 180 syllabus, then we'll compare notes.

Mark this syllabus up! What's important on here?

CE 180—Elementary Statics

Instructor:	James Finlay
Office:	Jacobs Hall, Rm. 620, 662-8537
E-mail:	suspsn@bridge
TA:	John A. Roebling
Office:	Jacobs Hall, Rm. 166B (no phone)
E-mail:	brooklyn@bridge
Class:	MWF 8:10–9:00, Rm. 328, Minami Hall

Textbook:	*Vector Mechanics for Engineers*, 5th Ed., by Clifford Paine
Homework:	Assigned on Fridays and must be turned in the following Friday
Help sessions:	Wed., 3:00–5:00 P.M.
Office hrs.:	By appt. only

Topics to be covered:	By:
1. Introduction	9/10
2. Forces in a Plane and Space	9/17
3. Equivalent System of Forces	9/24
TEST 1, WED., SEPT. 29	
4. Equilibrium in 2-D and 3-D	10/08
5. Centroids of Lines, Areas, and Volumes	10/22
TEST 2, WED., OCT. 27	
6. Analysis of Structures	11/05
7. Friction	11/12
TEST 3, WED., NOV. 17	
8. Moment of Inertia of Areas and Masses	12/02
Review	

COMPREHENSIVE FINAL EXAM, WED., DEC. 16, 2 P.M.

Grading:

Homework	20%
Project	5%
Tests	45%
Final exam	30%

Honor Code:
  Applies to all tests, the exam, and the project. You may work together on
  homework assignments, but copying is not permitted.

A. Fun with phonetics.

Do you know how to pronounce your professor's name? Professor Finlay who pronounces his name Fin-lee' isn't terribly hard to remember, but pronouncing Professor Xudong Liu (Z-Dong Lew) might be a bit tough if you forget to write it down.

B. Drop-ins welcome?

Make note of how to contact your professor should you need help, want to discuss a test, or need to get a drop card signed.

C. The teaching assistant (TA).

Does the professor prefer that you take homework questions to the TA rather than ask him or her?

D. Don't buy the wrong book!

Because engineering textbooks can be so expensive, many students purchase used texts from upperclassmen or student organizations. Before buying used texts, however, make sure that the text you get is being used in the class. Different editions often rearrange topics and have different exercises and problems.

E. Help!

Do you already have a lab on Wednesdays from 2:00 to 5:00 P.M.? Talk to your professor if you have an *academic* conflict (intramurals don't count) with any offered help sessions or office hours.

F. Check the amount of material to be covered in the noted time frames.

Chapter One (Introduction) is only 15 pages, most of it review—no problem. Chapter Five, however, might be 70 pages and it is covered in only two weeks. Flip through your textbook to become aware of when the material will be more comprehensive and time-consuming, and adjust your own schedule and priorities accordingly.

G. Put 'em on the calendar right away!

These kinds of surprises aren't fun.

H. Note how much everything is worth.

A quick calculation from this syllabus will tell you that each homework set is worth 2 percent of your total grade. When the going gets tough and there's too much due at one time in too many classes, make your trade-offs in the classes where you'll get penalized the least.

I. Professor irks, quirks, and policies.

Most professors will tell you what they appreciate and what bothers them on the first day of class. Make note of the attendance policy and any other "rules." Some professors will request that you hand in problem sets at their offices instead of bringing them to class. Others may even request that you sit in the exact same lecture hall seat for the whole semester so that they can learn and remember *all* 113 of your names. As funny or uptight as some of these requests may seem, do honor them.

What Am I in for?

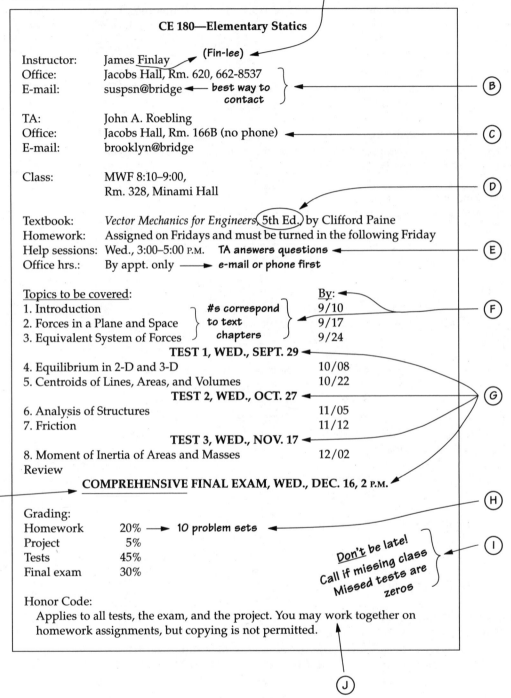

Ⓐ

CE 180—Elementary Statics

Instructor:	James Finlay *(Fin-lee)*
Office:	Jacobs Hall, Rm. 620, 662-8537
E-mail:	suspsn@bridge ◄— *best way to contact*

Ⓑ

TA:	John A. Roebling
Office:	Jacobs Hall, Rm. 166B (no phone)
E-mail:	brooklyn@bridge

Ⓒ

Class:	MWF 8:10–9:00, Rm. 328, Minami Hall

Ⓓ

Textbook:	*Vector Mechanics for Engineers,* 5th Ed. by Clifford Paine
Homework:	Assigned on Fridays and must be turned in the following Friday
Help sessions:	Wed., 3:00–5:00 P.M. *TA answers questions* ◄
Office hrs.:	By appt. only ——► *e-mail or phone first*

Ⓔ

Topics to be covered: By: ◄

1. Introduction   *#s correspond*   9/10
2. Forces in a Plane and Space   *to text*   9/17
3. Equivalent System of Forces   *chapters*   9/24

TEST 1, WED., SEPT. 29 ◄

4. Equilibrium in 2-D and 3-D   10/08
5. Centroids of Lines, Areas, and Volumes   10/22

TEST 2, WED., OCT. 27 ◄

6. Analysis of Structures   11/05
7. Friction   11/12

TEST 3, WED., NOV. 17 ◄

8. Moment of Inertia of Areas and Masses   12/02
Review

COMPREHENSIVE FINAL EXAM, WED., DEC. 16, 2 P.M.

Ⓕ

Ⓖ

Ⓚ

Ⓗ

Grading:

Homework	20% ——►	*10 problem sets* ◄
Project	5%	
Tests	45%	
Final exam	30%	

Don't be late!
Call if missing class
Missed tests are zeros

Ⓘ

Honor Code:
   Applies to all tests, the exam, and the project. You may work together on
   homework assignments, but copying is not permitted.

Ⓙ

J. Am I cheating?

If the syllabus or the school does not *spell out* what constitutes cheating, ask the professor. The university's honor code can be interpreted differently by different professors. Because you were able to compare answers in one class does not mean you are permitted to do so in all your classes. In engineering classes (especially computer science) there are a lot of gray areas that must be clarified for your own protection and understanding.

K. "Comprehensive" means everything.

No forgetting anything after the tests; everything must be *retained!* Some courses will not have cumulative exams, so enjoy these breaks and use all the extra mind space for other classes.

LAB PERIODS AND THE LAW OF LABS

Engineers have a lot of laboratory periods, sometimes as many as four a week during certain semesters or quarters. Lab classes enable us engineers to make the connection between the theory taught in class and the application used in practice. Labs are an opportunity to test our brilliant abilities in creative problem solving and help determine how much we've learned in class, and, ho hum . . . yes, how well we follow directions.

Freshman year the labs will be in the introductory sciences: Chemistry, Physics, and maybe some computer work and/or Biology. Later the lab classes will correspond to your introductory engineering and discipline-specific classes. The important thing to remember is, if you follow the directions:

The Results to Laboratory Experiments Are Completely Predictable
(and it's really difficult to screw up)

This is the *Law of Labs*, and it applies to all undergraduate engineering experiments. Of course, you might not look at your watch often enough and your beakered liquid crystallizes instead of merely turning pink, but that's your fault. If it's not your fault (which will happen), the TA will usually take pity, then help determine the problem, and often provide a remedy or "better" data to use for the write-up.

Although predictability makes it fairly easy to do well in these experimental labs, just how much you get out of these periods is completely up to you. Laboratory periods can be standing marathons that also test your patience, but don't let them be a waste of time.

- ☺ *Skim the lab before going.* Knowing exactly what must be accomplished for the experiment helps you recognize little problems before they become big problems, what dangers may be encountered (uh oh . . . I think I burned a hole in my sleeve), and how the experiment ties in with theory and scientific history.
- ☺ *Ace those lab quizzes!* Lab quizzes exist to ensure that you know what is going on when you come to lab. Doing well on them usually only requires you to pay attention in lecture and skim the lab manual.
- ☺ *Have a rotating group data transcriber.* It's easy to go into a lab session, write down numbers that are called out to you, and leave the laboratory without any real idea of what happened with the experiment. On the other hand, keeping track of data for one trial gives you a head start on how well the data will match theory when you write up the report. Catching a funky number in lab, with a TA there to explain it, is preferable to thinking it is an error after you get home. Lab sessions are much more entertaining—and educational—when you get to do everything.
- ☺ *Write in your lab manual.* If your lab manual is wordy, highlight key instructions. Write results, helpful hints from your TA, and your lab partner's full name and phone number—anything and everything you'd rather not lose and will need when writing up the report or results when you get home. Studying for laboratory exams is made easier by flipping through the note-supplemented manual at the end of the semester instead of going through each lab to determine and memorize the theory, applications, and results.
- ☺ *Be nice to your TAs.* They are students, too. Most TAs are graduate students or upperclassmen majoring in the department of your laboratory. They can relate to and remember the frustration of dud experiments or spending an afternoon or weekend on a circuit design or computer program that just won't work. The subject is what interests them, so don't be bashful about asking questions or going to their office hours.

Don't forget that introductory classes are rumored to be weed-outs (in both engineering and premed). The first few years may challenge you. Some of the required engineering classes may not even be in your major *or to your liking*, which makes studying and keeping up difficult. But don't be intimidated or frustrated by this; think of it as exercise for the mind and as stamina building—the curriculum for the versatile and well-rounded engineer. After the storm, the calm (and sun!) will come.

If you really do think your place in life is not as an engineer, make your decision to go "non-tech" because you suffer from a general lack of interest in problem solving and technical fields. Excellent engineers and other professionals with engineering degrees were not always the best engineering students.

Don't worry about your difficulties with mathematics, I assure you that mine are still greater.

—ALBERT EINSTEIN
German-American physicist (1879–1955), in a letter to a student

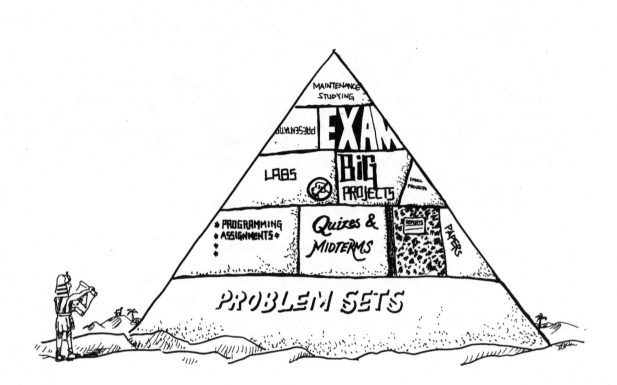

CHAPTER 7

Outside the Classroom— Workload and Studying

So you've been warned about the workload. Lots of work and unfortunately (fortunately?) there isn't much time for maintenance—you know, the day-to-day studying that reinforces the homework sets and class lectures. What makes engineering hard and so much work, of course, *is* the workload: problem sets, lab reports, and projects. There is always work to do, but the bulk of the work in engineering often hits in a tidal wave around the middle of the term. Everything is due at once. Midterms and tests seem to fall routinely in the same week. So, unless you like slam cramming, maintenance studying is important.

Maintenance studying for engineers is quite a bit different than that for our counterparts in liberal arts. Let's define maintenance studying as the time spent reading the text or reviewing class notes enough to know what is going on in class. With an English Literature class, you can understand the lecture without to having read the book, even make a few intelligent comments (just make comments on other comments, right?). In engineering, on the other hand, you get so busy doing the assigned problems that looking at notes or skimming ahead in the text often doesn't happen. Sometimes this works out, but usually skipping on maintenance results in transcribing lecture notes without really understanding what's going on.

PROBLEM SETS

Problem sets are a way of life for engineers. It is most likely that you will complete *at least* one problem set each week of your engineering education and for some quarters or semesters this number could climb to six or more per week. Problem sets can be of the homemade handout genre, questions assigned from the text, or random problems your professor may have you download from the class web site.

Problem sets define the busy work of engineers. While our nonengineering friends may claim they have just as much to do (reading assignments), the difference is that poli sci students can skip a reading (or several) and still do

well in the course, but skipping one problem set greatly reduces an engineer's chance of pulling an A. *To do well in your engineering classes, you must do the assigned problem sets, whether the professor collects them or not.* While the frequency and relentlessness of problem sets can be stressful and tiresome, there *are* some good aspects.

The Bright Side of Problem Sets

1. They teach you what you need to know. Learning material while doing problem sets saves you from having to power-absorb the material later on, before a test.
2. Doing a problem set is always better than writing a paper.
3. Problem sets make great practice problems for tests.

4. They force you to solve problems and communicate the results clearly and logically.
5. You get to know your classmates through answer-checking phone networks and late night peer help sessions.
6. You really do learn a lot.
7. You have a valid excuse to get out of annoying social engagements.

OK, you've bought a pad of the fab green engineering paper, some nice mechanical pencils, a big eraser, and an antislip cork-bottomed metal ruler. Now let's quickly go through the elements of a problem set and a solved problem:

The Format of the Problem Set

Assignment	Course number & title, section	Name, date	# / total

From the problem statement:

Given: Paraphrase the problem.

Find: List all the variables to be solved and questions to be answered.

Diagram and data: Draw a sketch of the system, labeling all relevant information from the problem statement. List the provided data needed to solve the problem. The data can be quantitative (i.e., $T=74°F$) or qualitative (i.e., converging-diverging nozzle).

Showing off your work:

Assumptions: Briefly state the assumptions you used to simplify and/or solve the problem. For example, if you were solving for how long it took for a watermelon to fall from a 2,000-foot-high building, an assumption might be: Air resistance was assumed to be negligible.

Analysis: Using the data and your assumptions—solve the problem! Start with the governing equation(s) and progress logically through the problem. Add comments that might explain choices, external information used (such as charts or tables), and how you manipulated equations. The grader should be able to logically follow your work.

Final answer: Box or double-underline the answer. Don't forget units!

Sample Problem

Problem 2.15

Given: Figure 2-15 shows a circuit whose elements have the following values

$\mathcal{E}_1 = 3V \qquad \mathcal{E}_2 = 5V$

$R_1 = 2\Omega \qquad R_2 = 4\Omega$

Find: a) the currents in all branches

b) the potential difference between points a and b

Assumptions: Current directions shown in figure.

Analysis:

a) Using Kirchhoff's junction rule at a: $(\Sigma i_{in} = \Sigma i_{out})$

$$i_3 = i_1 + i_2 \qquad\qquad (1)$$

Using Kirchhoff's loop rule:

Left loop ccw starting at a

$$-i_1R_1 - \mathcal{E}_1 - i_1R_1 + \mathcal{E}_2 + i_2R_2 = 0$$
$$-2i_1R_1 + i_2R_2 = \mathcal{E}_1 - \mathcal{E}_2 \qquad\qquad (2)$$

Right loop cw from a

$$+i_3R_1 - \cancel{\mathcal{E}_2} + i_3R_1 + \cancel{\mathcal{E}_2} + i_2R_2 = 0$$
$$i_2R_2 + 2i_3R_1 = 0 \qquad\qquad (3)$$

Solving 3 equations for 3 unknowns:

$$(1)\ i_3 = i_1 + i_2 \ \rightarrow \ i_1 = i_3 - i_2$$

Plug (1) into (2):

$$-2(i_3 - i_2)R_1 - \mathcal{E}_1 + \mathcal{E}_2 + i_2R_2 = 0$$
$$-2R_1i_3 + (2R_1 + R_2)i_2 = \mathcal{E}_1 - \mathcal{E}_2 \qquad\qquad (4)$$

Solve for i_2 in (3) and plug into (4)

$$-2R_1(i_3) + \left(\frac{-2i_3R_1}{R_2}\right)(2R_1 + R_2) = \mathcal{E}_1 - \mathcal{E}_2$$

Solve for i_3:

$$i_3 = \frac{(\mathcal{E}_2 - \mathcal{E}_1)R_2}{4R_1(R_1 + R_2)} = \frac{(5V - 3V)(\cancel{4\Omega})}{\cancel{4}(2\Omega)(2 + 4)\cancel{\Omega}} = 0.167A \ \rightarrow \ \boxed{i_3 = 0.167A}$$

Plug $i_3 = 0.167A$ into (2) to solve for i_2:

$$i_2 = -\frac{\mathcal{E}_2 - \mathcal{E}_1}{2(R_1 + R_2)} = -\frac{(5V - 3V)}{2(2 + 4)\Omega} = -0.167A \qquad \boxed{i_2 = -0.167A}$$

Solving (1)

$$i_1 = i_3 - i_2 = 0.167A - (-0.167A)$$
$$= 0.33A \qquad\qquad \boxed{i_1 = 0.33A}$$

b) Potential difference $= V_a - V_b$

$$V_a - i_2R_2 - \mathcal{E}_2 = V_b$$
$$V_a - V_b = i_2R_2 + \mathcal{E}_2$$
$$= (-0.167A)(4\Omega) + 5V$$
$$= 4.33V \qquad\qquad \boxed{V_a - V_b = 4.33V}$$

Of course, you need not follow this entire routine for a problem set in, say, calculus or physics. It is generally reserved for engineering classes where the problems present situations that require decision making based on assumptions. When time is tight, everything can be shortened and paraphrased.

OK—here are some things that make problem sets less of a burden:

1. *Look for a subject study guide or a problem-solver book for the tough classes.* English majors have *Cliff* (or *Coles* for the Canucks) notes, and engineers have *Schaum's. Schaum's Outline Series* and *REA's Problem Solvers* are great resources for both completing assignments and studying for tests. The exact same problem you may be working on can sometimes be found in these books. Although most university bookstores carry engineering course outline books, school libraries often have copies, too.

2. *Check the back of the textbook for answers.* Don't be the sad and sorry student who struggles through the whole semester before realizing the author has included in an appendix the answers to check your solutions to chapter problems.

> ⚠ **Beware!** The answers in the back of the textbook are not always correct. If you are confident you have solved a problem correctly and it checks out with other perplexed classmates, but not the book, you are probably right and the book wrong.

3. *Look for textbook example problems and problems that weren't assigned (but have solutions in the back) that might give clues to the tough problems.* Even though the problems are different, there may be a common method or a hint that isn't obvious in the assigned problem.

4. *Get old problem sets from upperclassmen.* Test problems often come from the problem sets of previous years'.

5. *Look at problem sets early.* Not necessarily to *do* the problem set, but to take a quick inventory of how hard it appears to be, how much time it will take, and if there is any material that may send you to the professor's or TA's office for assistance.

☞ A Note on Problem Set Shortcuts

Shortcuts offer the fastest way to get from one place to another. So, the fastest way to get a problem set completed is to get a few pointers from the TA, a few hints from a friend, and some close examples from the textbook. With many bits of help, it is often possible to get the problem set finished *without* really understanding the material. Shortcuts should be used to keep yourself sane . . . and that can be OK when you are in the middle of midterms and your roommate is circulating a petition demanding that you do your laundry, *but* the central purpose of problem sets is to learn the material. As a student, however, your goal is often just to get them done, so make things easier on yourself—use problem sets to learn the material. If you're having a bad week, make time later to go back and understand what you missed. It will make for a much more benign exam week.

6. *Don't waste time pulling your hair out—see the TA.* If you have worked, reworked, and re-reworked and your answers still aren't checking out, then it's time to make an appointment with the TA. You don't have time to wait for a revelation.

7. *Find a classmate with whom you work well.* Two working together seems to be the optimum number for completing and understanding required assignments. Working with another engineering student also offers an additional perspective when tackling problems that require some creativity. Teaching material to someone else also ensures that you understand it.

PROGRAMS

If you are a computer science major, your programming assignments may far outnumber your problem sets. All engineering students take at least one Programming class. To many, computer science is an engaging challenge—a return to logical and creative problem solving. To others, programming is a frustrating game.

Good programmers are patient. They are persistent. They have to be. Every new program to write can look like a distant mountain to climb with the summit hidden in clouds. Even those who love programming say that there is a wall you hit every time. But given some time, patience, and persistence, the *Aha!* comes.

- ☺ *Make variable names obvious.* Be as descriptive as possible. Short variable names may be more pleasant to type, but they are much more difficult to keep track of when debugging your program.
- ☺ *Look for different perspectives.* Ask for different explanations of difficult concepts or problems.
- ☺ *Comment. Comment. Comment.* Commenting your code ensures that you and the grader understands what you are doing. Have fun with it.
- ☺ *RTFM.* Read the foolish manual (or something like that . . .).
- ☺ *Be elegant.* If your program works, how can you get a low grade? Think about it this way: You could build a crooked bookshelf from old splintering boards or you could build a beautiful teak bookshelf sanded to perfection. Both hold books. Which one would you want?
- ☺ *Planning puts you in touch with your inner program.* Coding without a plan can be disastrous. Before you jump into coding, sit down and plan out your structure on a piece or paper. Make an outline and write pseudocode. Experienced programmers often use these notes as the comments in their program.

LAB REPORTS

Laboratory classes and their reports can be highly time consuming with seemingly little payoff. Although lab reports can take way too long to prepare and are often worth fewer units than a regular class (for which you spend far less time doing outside work), lab periods and experiments can be cool because you

actually get to see the application of all the taught theory and scientific law. It's a chance to see how things really work instead of reading how they should work.

You remember the first law of labs: *The results of laboratory experiments are completely predictable.* Now consider its corollary:

If you understand the theory behind the experiments, lab classes are an easy A.

Think about it! How can you get anything less than an A when you already know the results *before* doing the experiment? After attending the lecture section of a lab and reading the directions, you could probably write the entire discussion section without the data because undergrad lab experiments always demonstrate some kind of engineering theory that is important for you to understand.

So why doesn't everyone get A's in lab classes? There are two ways to biff in lab classes:

1. Turning reports in late.
2. The write up ain't written too good.

Because lab reports *are* time sinks and often rank low priority on the assignment to do list, it's not hard to fall behind and end up handing your report in late. This isn't a big deal if you can make up labs at the end of the semester, but if you can't and points are deducted for late reports, you could be in trouble. Although it seems obvious, if you get behind on one report you will have to write two reports next week. Not a nice thought, eh? Remembering that should be enough to help you get the report in on time. However, too many students get stuck consistently handing in late reports (with points off) when they are actually working at the *same rate* as the students who are getting them in on time.

Points docked off pleasantly punctual lab reports are usually given for careless errors: minute things that seem really obvious but are often overlooked when you are hurriedly trying to turn out a lab report before the 5:00 P.M. deadline.

- ☺ *Don't use pronouns!* No no no (unless your odd-duck teacher says it's OK). Also, the standard voice for engineering lab reports is passive although many professors no longer require it. Sentences such as "Then I measured the outer diameter of the spherical tank" should be "A measurement of the spherical tank's outer diameter was then taken."
- ☺ *Type and save your lab reports.* Even though typing a report with proper subscripts, superscripts, notations, and equations is time-consuming, it goes much faster after the first one.
- ☺ *Follow directions.* Did you answer all the questions? At some schools, the question section of the report is the most rigorous and important part.

☞ **On the subject of tardy reports.** If it looks like you absolutely can't get a report in on time (it happens to everyone at some point), call or E-mail your TA and ask for an extension. Explain what else is going on in your life that is preventing you from completing it. Calling is better than sending E-mail because the TA can hear your pain. The TA sympathy factor tends to be directly dependent on the amount of time *before* the submission deadline that you contact them.

- ☺ *Harass the TA until you do understand.*
- ☺ *Run spell check and reread.* It's a hassle . . . you are tired, but spelling mistakes are badd, typoa worse, and misuse is not so good two.
- ☺ *Label everything.* Tables, diagrams, and especially charts and plots. Take a look at the neglected graph below. What's missing? Go ahead and write on the page.

An Unlabeled Plot

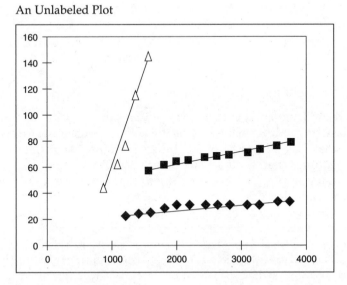

A lot is missing! This is how a good lookin' plot ought to look.

The Labeled Plot

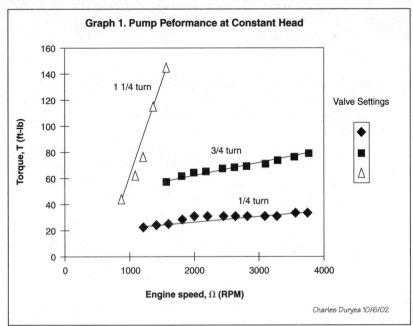

Software to get the job done

- Word processing program with an equation editor. Pretty good ones: Microsoft Word or Corel Word Perfect.
- Spreadsheet program for data manipulation (when there is a lot of it), nice tables, and slick graphs. Pretty good ones: Corel Quattro Pro, Microsoft Excel, or Lotus 1-2-3.

It's tough to remember it all, isn't it? Check out "A Quick Guide to Slick Graphs" on pages 74–75 to make sure you got it all.

The Overachiever's Lab Format

The format and length of the required lab report can vary from year to year and class to class, depending on how it was done when your professor went to college and what little things he or she thinks are most beneficial to you. Vital components of the well thought out lab are usually covered in the first class of the semester or quarter. The following format illustrates a good way to go if your professors don't spell out what they want.

> **Use the first lab as a template.** After you write the first lab for a class—save it to disk and use it as a template for the rest of the quarter or semester. Typing over labs saves mucho time formatting and inserting Greek symbols for variables.

0. Cover Page
   Include the title of the lab, the lab number, the date submitted, the class title and course number, the names of any group members, the professor's name, the TA's name, your name, and your E-mail address.

I. Introduction
   A. Abstract, Statement of Purpose, or Brief Summary
      The first section or statement should simply state what the purpose of the experiment is and how the experiment will be observed or studied. A statement of purpose is usually a few sentences long, whereas an abstract or brief summary can be a paragraph or two. The abstract summarizes the entire experiment, the importance of the experiment, and the results.

> **Who is your audience?** Introductions (and even the whole report) can vary greatly depending on the audience for whom you are writing. References disagree about who you should assume your readers are: peers (classmates) or professionals (as if you were a practicing engineer). Ask your TA or professor, but keeping things in perspective, your best bet is to write for a single nitpicky grader who is pretending to be uninformed regarding the experiment and results.

B. Definition of Variables

Define all the variables used in calculations and discussion. Variables are listed in alphabetical order with Greek symbols first. Appendix A lists the Greek alphabet so you can even get those in the right order!

Do the Definition of Variables section last. It can be more time efficient to wait to do this section after keeping a running list of the variables as you use them in the write-up and calculations. It saves time having to flip through your notes and then going back to add the ones you missed.

Rearrange your desktop tool bars. Set up your word processor or spreadsheet tool bars to include frequent use buttons (like superscript and subscript) that aren't already there.

II. Background
A. Equipment Setup

List the *main* equipment (rulers, pencils, and so forth can be assumed). Give enough detail so the reader has an idea how to reproduce the experiment. If an equipment list is already in your lab manual, just copy it. The following are acceptable:

Anemometer

DC Power Supply, 0-40V

These, of course, are better:

Mini Anemometer, Kurtz series 490, Model 490, 0-200 or 0-2000 SFPM, ±1.25%

DC Power Supply, HP LVR series, Model 6266B, 0-40V, 0-5A, ±0.1%

Yes, slightly geeky, but there is a reason. If later researchers wanted to duplicate your results, they wouldn't want to use any old anemometer or power supply, but one as similar as possible to what you used in order to minimize deviations.

B. Experimental Method

This should already be in your lab manual. All you have to do is convert it to passive voice and your own words. If it isn't in your manual, remember to take good notes during the experiment. The easiest and clearest way to express the method is in numbered steps.

Number your equations. Number all the useful equations you mention in your lab. Just like in textbooks, numbering makes it easy to refer to the equations in the discussion section instead of typing out the proper name.

When time is tight, write equations in by hand. Although both Microsoft Word and Word Perfect have good equation editors, they can be slow to use. When you are running close to the wire, consider leaving a few blank lines and writing the equations in by hand.

C. **Theory**

What are the governing equations that describe this experiment? Again, these should be in your lab manual; if not, just pull them from a textbook.

III. **Results and Calculations**

A. **Results**

Results can be quantitative and/or qualitative. If you have a whole truckload of raw quantitative data, it should be placed in an appendix that is referenced from the results section. A moderate amount of quantitative data can be included in a table in this section. *However, what TAs and professors most want to see in this section are some slick graphs that show how all the data correlates to theory.* A graph says a thousand words, raw data doesn't say much of anything. Check out "A Quick Guide to Slick Graphs" to make just that.

A Quick Guide to Slick Graphs

Another engineer should be able to pick up a slick graph and be able to completely understand what the graph is showing without knowing anything about the lab experiment. Let's go to our labeled Graph 1 to look at the main points of slick graphing.

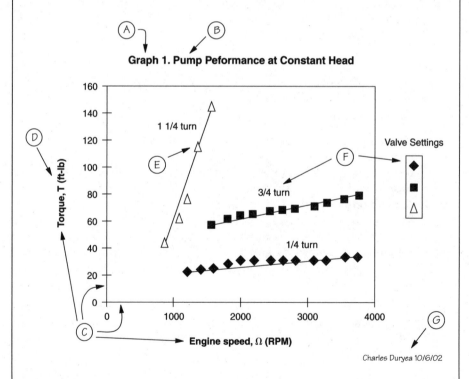

Graph 1. Pump Peformance at Constant Head

Charles Duryea 10/6/02

A. **Label**

Labeling, like numbering your equations, makes for easy reference and a polished report.

B. **Title**

The title should briefly say what was going on that produced the results displayed by the graph. Don't restate the axes! "Torque vs. Engine Speed" sounds like a boxing match, not a graph title. Capital letters should occur as with any title.

C. **Variables**

The independent variable is usually plotted on the *abscissa* or horizontal axis, while the dependent variable is plotted on the *ordinate* or vertical axis. Thus, torque is on the ordinate because it is was the result of our fiddling with the engine speed. When dealing with non-dimensional or dimensional, the axes should be consistent; that is, make both axes non-dimensional or both dimensional. Label the axis with the variable and abbreviations or symbol (if there is one).

D. **Variable units**

Don't forget them! If you have a quantity that is dimensionless, label it so with "dimensionless."

E. **Points, lines, curves, etc.**

If you have experimental data, the data points must be shown. While Mardi Gras point colors look snazzy on the computer screen, it is better to convert the default multicolored boxes over to symbols if you are printing on a black-and-white printer. Once printed, it will be much easier to differentiate groupings and see the overlap. Lines and curves through data are usually "best fits" (not connect-the-dots) with a ruler or french curve. Best fits can be done by eye or for linear correlation by using a regression formula (easy with a spreadsheet). Do use an appropriate best fit; while a 9th order polynomial fit might go through all the points, it would not represent the theory at all! The best-fit line or curve through data is a solid line. Dashed lines are usually saved for extrapolation (when the line is extended beyond the collected data). When you have multiple lines for comparative data, this standard is ignored so you are able to differentiate lines.

F. **Legend or callouts**

Labels to differentiate data are necessary with more than one set. A legend off to the side or callouts that label the data on the graph can be used. The fewer words used, the better.

G. **Signature and date**

Some professors ask students to sign and date all of the graphs they produce and submit.

B. **Sample Calculations**

Include an example of each calculation you performed in processing your results. All the equations should be referenced or follow directly from the background theory section. Include any assumptions you made.

C. **Error or Uncertainty Analysis**

"Error? I just followed the directions . . . " Error is the difference between the measured value and the accepted or "true value" given by theory. For experimental analysis in lab reports, error is usually represented numerically as a percentage or as a magnitude ± the measured value. Error can also be represented graphically with range markers shown with the graphed data.

Error using inadequate data is much less than those using no data at all.
—CHARLES BABBAGE, English inventor/mathematician (1792–1871)

IV. Discussion

A. Discussion of Results

State what you learned—or were supposed to learn—from your results. Make statements that describe correlations and reference a graph or plot in the Results section: "From Graph (2), it can be seen that output torque increases with input power." Remember the Law of Labs—don't worry if your discussion section is short—all you are doing is stating experimental correlations that prove well-known theory.

B. Error

After calculating error or uncertainty to your heart's content (maybe more), you now get to *discuss* it. Since it is unlikely that the only errors in the experiment were due to instrument inexactness, you need to mention possible sources of added error that may have affected your results. One sentence explaining which error(s) occurred and how is usually sufficient. Engineers have distinguished several types of errors on which we can place blame for our imperfection:

1. **Random.** No idea how it messed up. Although you have no idea what happened, speculate.
2. **Systematic.** It consistently messed up about the same every time. Example: Your watch is 10 minutes fast, so every time you make a time check, it is +10 minutes off.
3. **Human.** You messed up. Example: You misread the ruler.
4. **Computation.** The device or instrument used to crunch numbers messed up. Example: You are calculating the distance to the fourth nearest galaxy with 327,682,357,883,567 significant digits and your computer only can handle 256. This error is rare for our little labs.

If your data and results are really all over the place, the best thing to do is discuss the expected results for the experiment and then, with the aid of our four types of error, surmise what happened.

C. Questions from Lab Manual

Some professors will have you put them here. Others will have you put them in an appendix.

V. Conclusion

Based on the results, state what was proven. The conclusion should answer all the questions that came to mind from reading the experiment's purpose.

"In conclusion . . . " isn't a good way to start the conclusion section. But you already knew that.

VI. Appendixes, Bibliography
Appendixes can include raw data, error calculations, answers to assigned questions, and extra diagrams or plots. Bibliographies are the same as for papers in any discipline.

Author's last name, first name. <u>Book/Paper title</u>. City: Publisher, ©.

Example:

Donaldson, K. <u>The Engineering Student Survival Guide</u>, 1st ed. Burr Ridge, IL: McGraw-Hill, 1999.

So there you have it—the most complete lab report possible. Depending on the amount of detail required by your professor, lab reports can range from a few pages of data and comments to 30 or more pages. It is highly unlikely that your professor will require you to go through all the steps outlined above, but if he or she does, you should be in good shape.

A final note on labs. Don't get caught up in little details. Producing a good lab report is already a lot of work, so don't waste even more time fiddling with colored plots, scanned-in photographs, overcomplicated CAD[1] drawings, and so on.

PROJECTS

Engineering projects pop up in any course where there may be some engineering design going on (almost everywhere). Whether you choose door 1 (a heat exchanger!) or door 2 (you, too, could design your very *own* voltmeter!), recognize that projects always take more time than is budgeted. The key to painless projects is: *Start early*. Not a surprise, eh? We will subdivide projects into two categories: SPPs and BTUs. SPPs (small, piddly projects) and BTUs (big term undertakings) can be individual or group projects.

Small, Piddly Projects (SPPs)

SPPs are those projects that professors decide are fun ways for you to apply what you've learned in their courses. You often have only two weeks (or less) toward the end of the term to wrack your brain, then write your work up nicely, and maybe even present it to the class.

1. *First things first.* Understand the project assignment. Many times the problem statement is much more confusing than the problem itself.
2. *Research.* SPPs usually do not require much outside research . . . unless paying attention in class isn't your forte. Are there any back-of-the-textbook computer programs you need to learn? Depending on the project, sometimes a quick trip to the library or a 15-minute Web search can help substantially.

---

[1]CAD (Computer Aided Design) refers to any drawings, modelings, or renderings done on a computer typically with software specific for that purpose.

Once you figure out what you need to do, what equations you'll need, what methods work best, and what kind of results you should expect, you are set to . . .

3. *Work it.* Allow yourself lots of time (goes with starting early) for computations and problem solving. Plug through it. If you need to write a computer program, don't forget to allow time for debugging and sanity breaks.

4. *Test it.* Does everything work without glitches? Your work should be easy for the professor to follow when he or she grades it. Did you state your assumptions? Sometimes decisions that are clearly evident to us are not obvious to others tackling the same design problem. Look critically at your project for any potential holes that could cost you.

5. *Fix things.* Rework it. Add. Subtract. When running short on time, fill in as much as possible and list what you might have done had you not run out of time.

6. *Write it up.* Isn't it exciting? You are almost finished.

7. *Go the extra mile.* It takes very little time to polish up a project. Throw all those sources into a bibliography. Draw a diagram that clarifies final concepts. Whip out a spreadsheet graph. Number your pages.

Big Term Undertakings (BTUs)

And you thought BTUs were British thermal units! You just can't unknowingly and accidently find yourself in a class with a term project (a.k.a. big undertaking). A BTU is not an SPP with more time to think. You should have been forewarned by upperclassmen and even by professors. Big term undertakings are often the finale—the end of a course series or maybe the end of your undergrad career (senior projects!). They tend to reflect real-life engineering and project management. Although BTUs are a *lot* of work, it is cool to see the engineering theory you've learned come together to produce something impressive. A good term project will make you an expert in your chosen topic.

1. *First things first.* Understand the project assignment and what is expected. Master the acronyms. Learn (or relearn) how to do journal searches at the library, operate machine-shop tools, use computer codes you have tried to forget, and so forth.

☞ **Eeny meeny miny mo.** If you are able to pick your own term project topic, decide as early as possible! Choose something you really like. Besides consuming your life, it could maybe even lead to a job or graduate work.

---

2. *Research.* It is this phase of the BTU that consumes the largest chunk of time; as much as half of the term can be spent getting up to speed on the assigned or chosen topic. Any good project that really puts you to work will cause anxiety and frustration early on. The whitecapped swell of frustration follows the realization-of-the-magnitude-of-what-you-have-gotten-yourself-into wave that washes over you as you weed through all the background information. *First,* start with the easy stuff. If you are doing a project on

contaminant tracking in rivers, begin with some water quality and contaminant readings from an environmental engineering text. After you get that nailed down, move on to the journal articles. Don't be afraid to ask questions of professors, graduate students, friends of distant relatives, and even people in industry.

3. *Generate.* Generate as many ideas, solutions, methods, possibilities and paths as possible. This is a great time for a mind map (see page 81).

4. *Work it.* Working it means decision making by you and perhaps a computer. After the time and toil devoted to research, this step is almost disappointingly easy.

5. *Double-check results.* Does everything make sense? Check your assumptions. Double-check your constants and anything that involves a unit conversion. The answers are often obviously good or bad for BTUs. If you find everything looks good, it's time to feel *relief.* If things look monstrous, make an appointment with the professor—there may still be time to recover. You are approaching the home stretch.

6. *Tend to the small details.* With big projects there are often many minor considerations that get tossed aside. Dot your i's, cross your t's. Produce a schematics of your solution and process. Go back and fill in the gaps.

7. *Write it up.* After all the time you have devoted to this project, don't slack off now! Writing up the BTU will take more time, patience, and disk space than expected. If possible, get a good night's sleep before the final edit. It is painful to see a typo in the freshly bound copy.

8. *Go the extra mile.* Polish it up. Scan in pertinent photographs. "Borrow" some slick graphics from the Web (it's legal for educational purposes as long as you credit the source!). Generate some CAD drawings and renderings. Put a cool graphic on the cover page.

9. *Take it to the printer for binding and an extra copy.* Don't do this last minute! ("The earliest we can have this done for you is tomorrow afternoon.") Pick a cool color for the cover (Kinko's has Rocket Red for the Aero/Astros). Make an extra copy. Finish out the semester with a bang.

Group Projects

After a couple of years of being almost entirely self-reliant in the completion of problem sets, assignments, and labs, engineering students get thrown into groups. ("You mean I *have* to work with someone else?") Group projects often make their first appearance the junior or senior year in design classes, but at more hip schools they are assigned as early as the freshman year or for laboratory classes. Although it may feel completely unnatural to work with other people, engineers in industry almost always work as part of a team. Who could design and build a 727 aircraft single-handedly? Group projects add a whole new dimension to working on a project; everyone has different opinions, different schedules, different expectations, and different amounts of time and energy they are willing to commit. How should you tackle it?

1. *Choose a group leader.* Anarchy isn't usually a good thing. Flatter a responsible peer and nominate him or her. If you are interested in heading up your team, skip to number 8 and then come back. It is also a good idea to appoint a scribe at each meeting.

2. *Establish a timeline or—for larger projects—plan out your project on a Gantt chart.* The earlier the better. Keep it updated so that every group member is accountable and on schedule. For more about a Gantt chart, read the boxed material below.

Mr. Gantt Would Be So Pleased

A Gantt chart is a schedule represented in bar-graph form used to plan the sequence of project tasks over a known time period to ensure that all deadlines and important milestones are met appropriately. Tasks are listed down the vertical axis in sequential order, while time is listed in blocks across the top. According to engineering lore, Henry Gantt was able to boost World War I factory production because workers related better to a pictorial representation of project progress and goals.

For our wee project of building a dorm bedroom loft, the time is days. For most course projects, the time scale will be in weeks. Bar charts show the amount of time a task requires by spanning from the start date to the planned finish date. (A) A dotted line with a diamond (B) (····◇) extended from a bar is the float (or extra) time there may be until the task must be completed; that is, you want to have your wood purchased by Tuesday, but to get help from your visiting sister (a carpenter) it really needs to be purchased by Wednesday afternoon (B). Once you have started working on tasks, you can go back and update your chart by (C) filling in an equivalent percentage of the block. The (D) vertical dashed line represents the current day. (E) Dependencies are noted with arrows and (F) milestones are noted with a point.

The Gantt Chart for the Loft of Love

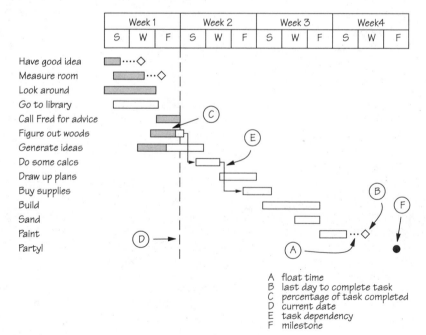

A float time
B last day to complete task
C percentage of task completed
D current date
E task dependency
F milestone

Phase 1: Define
    Get an idea of what you want
       to build.
    Measure your room.

Phase 2: Research
    Go look at other rooms with
       lofts.
    Look through *Architectural
       Digest.*
    Talk to some other handy
       people who have built a loft
       or two in past.
    Figure out what kind of wood
       you want.

Phase 3: Design
    Come up with lots of ideas.
    Do some quick statics
       calculations.
    Draw up master plans.

Phase 4: Build
    Buy the wood and hardware.
    Build.

Phase 5: Finish
    Sand.
    Paint.

Phase 6: Celebrate

3. *The mantra for brainstorming sessions is: Every idea is a good idea.* Remember that when you want to bang someone on the head with your binder. Write down every suggestion. Encourage wild ideas—the best thoughts can come from the most random inspirations.

The Marvelous Mind Map

Mind maps are an excellent tool for recording all the many directions and ideas of brainstorms. They can be used for individual or group creativity. Although the format can take any form you wish, the mind map usually starts with the central idea in the middle of the page (or flipchart) with other ideas and thoughts radiating outward. Mind maps are great for seeing recurring ideas and patterns.

Want an example? Keep reading!

4. *Divide up tasks.* Define and divide central and secondary tasks among your group members. Everyone should have one area for which they are responsible but also have multiple secondary tasks that assist other group members. Work with your team so that all members are matched with work they like.
5. *Keep a log book.* Write everything in it and don't lose it! Why? Go to top of page 82.
6. *During the research stage, use the first 10 to 15 minutes of each group meeting for a "round table."* The round table format allows everyone to explain briefly what they have done (battles fought and won) since the last meeting and any stumbling blocks (dragons) they may have hit. Many times one group member can help out or solve another's problem.
7. *Be a nice person to work with.* Pull your share. Volunteer to go first. Know when to shut up. Keep a sense of humor. Ask for the input from any quiet group members.
8. *Avoid being named to the leadership position unless you really love that kind of thing.* It is great experience, but the person in charge often ends up doing the most work.

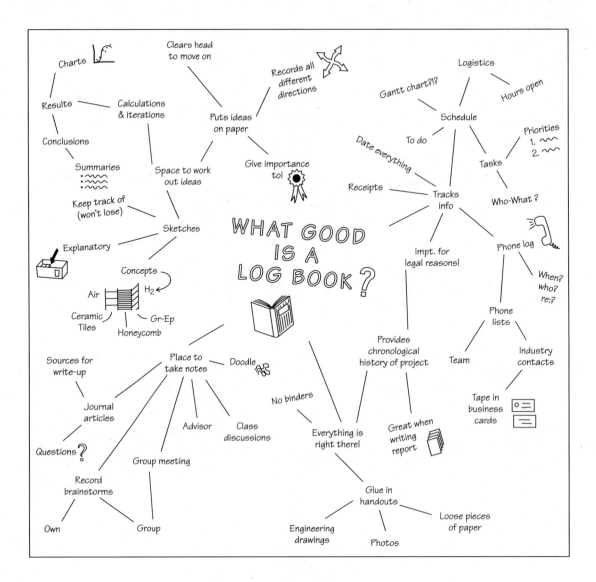

PRESENTATIONS

If you have to give an oral presentation, don't even consider doing it without overhead projectors or slides. First of all, talks are much easier when you have overheads with which to share the audience's attention. Second, good overheads or slides (especially color ones) make for a polished presentation that will be sure to earn you brownie points. Microsoft blessed us with Power Point, a simple-to-pick-up, user-friendly program that makes killer slides or overheads in almost no time.

If your professor has a specific format or outline he or she expects you to follow, simply fill in the blanks and use it. However if freelancing, consider some of the following presentation basics:

Software to get the job done. For overheads: Microsoft Power Point or any word-processing program that you can manipulate to print horizontally and insert graphics.

☺ *Put different topics on different slides.* One *text* slide per minute is a good rule of thumb. If you end up with 13 text slides for a five-minute talk, you have too many topics and need to reorganize!

☺ *Storyboard first.* Before you sit down at the computer, work out on paper what information and diagrams you want on each slide. Doing this actually saves time.

☺ *Slides should highlight the main points (not be a transcript) of the speaker's talk.* Details and minor points should be discussed by the speaker instead of crammed onto the slide. The fewer the words on the slide, the better.

☺ *Slide titles and bulleted text should have the same sentence structure.* It flows. It's cohesive.

☺ *A blank bright white screen mesmerizes audiences and clues them out.* When you're not using it, turn off the overhead projector or cover up the display with paper. The audience should be listening to you.

☺ *If you have many graphs or pictures, consider running two overhead or slide projectors simultaneously.* This is particularly effective when you have comparative graphs or data or a graphic that best accompanies a text slide.

☞ On your own? Here's the . . .

TYPICAL TECH TALK TOOL KIT

to be tweaked to your liking. It can be used for anything from a progress report to a final project presentation.

☺ *Title page.* Name, rank, serial number.

☺ *Overview of the talk.* The overview is generally a list in bullet format of the slide topics to follow. People like to know what is coming up.

☺ *Introduction.* Define the problem, briefly discuss the experiment, and state the goal(s).

☺ *Background.* What background information is pertinent to an understanding of this discussion? Include the main governing equation or central theory and assumptions.

☺ *Progress/accomplishments.* What have you (or your team) contributed? Show any pertinent charts, tables, and so forth. This is the presentation equivalent to the results and discussion sections of the lab report.

☺ *Conclusions.* What was discovered? What do your findings mean in the big scheme of things?

☺ *Questions left unanswered, areas for further research.* You really would have liked to further investigate some of these other areas, but time ran out. This is the place to mention stumbling blocks and future directions.

☺ *Acknowledgements.* Thanks to . . .

☺ *Rehearse!* It makes such a difference—to you and your audience. Great presentations have been ruined by poor speaking or fumbling to get slides in the right order. If you tend to get nervous giving oral presentations, try to think of your talk as an explanatory discussion with friends rather than a scripted narrative. Pretend you are a tour guide and let your slides cue you.

☺ *For formal presentations, distribute handouts with copies of your slides.* Power Point allows you to print multiple reductions of slides on a single page in the print menu. Any additional supporting material that, because of time constraints, did not make your presentation can also be included in the handouts.

PAPERS

Papers, optimistically believed to be rare in engineering education, are saved from extinction by the writing requirement. You may choose to fulfill the requirement with Post-Modern Ideals in Literature or Technical Writing. Whichever class you choose, pick what you like and will find useful, not what you think is easy. Writing on topics that don't interest you is not fun or easy. Not many of us will graduate and be granted a secretary as part of our first job package. Engineers in industry might find themselves devoting more time to business letters, memos, and reports than to computational work. Grad school doesn't let you escape either; there are many essays and proposals to write.

Freshman and sophomore engineering papers are lab reports, memos to fictitious companies, clients, or agencies, article summaries, and maybe an explanatory paper that accompanies an experiment or computer program. As an upperclassman, you may be assigned research papers that are rather like wordy lab reports under the guise of a paper.

Even though it is highly likely that you will need more help with a paper that is more than a lab report, that coaching is left to a different college survival guide—possibly one written by an English major.

MAINTENANCE STUDYING

Much study is a weariness of the flesh.
                    —Bible

What is there to study in engineering? Everything important is learned through problem sets, right? Not really. Only the practical knowledge is learned in problem sets, but really understanding cause and effect and the why and how comes from reading (yikes!) the text, looking over notes and problem sets as you get them back, and paying attention in class (or some combination of the above). Studying to understand what is going on in class is maintenance studying. Maintenance studying differs from test-tomorrow studying and how-do-I-do-this-homework-problem studying because it takes a higher level of motivation. Studying to learn and to understand happens for the truly inspired, but it can be difficult for the rest of us. Studying to keep up, though, never takes as long or is as painful as we might think it is.

Studying from the Textbook

Of course the shapes of these matrices must be properly matched—B and C have the same shape, so they can be added, and A and D are the right size for premultiplication and postmultiplication. The proof of this law is too boring for words.

GILBERT STRANG
American mathematician and professor,
from *Linear Algebra and Its Applications*

Engineering professors do not seem to depend as heavily on textbooks or outside readings as other instructors often do. Some professors will actually assign sections of the textbook to read; others will never mention the text at all (leaving you frustrated for wasting $80). For the most part, engineering textbooks are fairly good because they are fun to dust off later and reread (as references of course), but more importantly they provide the background and theory to pull seemingly random problems and concepts together.

So you have purchased, borrowed, or stolen the course text. What should you do with it?

1. *Read it*. Peruse it. Skim for boldface print. Even when the professor doesn't assign sections to read, use the index or table of contents to find the most

pertinent sections. Once you understand the reasoning behind one concept, you will see similarities in other concepts.

2. *Learn important terminology.* Understand the professor. Impress classmates. Woo the opposite sex.

3. *Work through example problems.* Homework and test problems will be much easier—*guaranteed.* Also try working through derivations without looking. When the text says"left as an exercise for the reader," do it! No one can teach you as well as you can teach yourself.

4. *Interact with it.* If this is a text you plan to keep, don't be afraid to mark it up. Make studying from a textbook proactive: Write comments in the margins, underline or highlight key phrases or terms, tab pages with useful charts and tables, and keep a list of questions to ask the TA. Proactive studying will keep you focused.

5. *Take notes from it.* Some folks find that to *really* absorb what they read, they need to take notes on the readings. However, time will not be available to take notes on all the sections you cover in class unless you are superhuman or need hobbies. However, taking notes from book material is extremely useful if you outline sections that have been difficult to understand or appear to be very important to the course.

   ☺ *Read the section first and then go back and take notes.* Taking notes as you read makes it more difficult to distinguish what material is important and you may write down much more than is necessary.

   ☺ *Do not redraw charts or diagrams; try to translate them into your own words.* You'll find that you will remember them better.

   ☺ *Write your book notes on one-side of loose-leaf paper.* With everything on one side, you can spread your notes out, and rearrange and even tape them to the bathroom wall without fear of missing material.

What to Do when the Textbook Stinks!

6. *Use it as a hot mat.* Perfect size with great thermal insulative properties. Unfortunately one needs only so many hot mats. Hmm . . . nothing more discouraging than a bad textbook. It's not hard to spot one because it often displays these characteristics: useless examples, not enough (helpful) examples, poor explanations of key concepts, too many words, and not enough pictures. So what do you do?

   ☺ *Look for a study guide.* Schaum's to the rescue again. (See page 68.)

   ☺ *Find another textbook in the same subject by*

a different author. Your school library is likely to have a plethora of texts on the same subject.

☺ *Ask an upperclassman for his or her old notes.* Offer same-day copy and return service.

☺ *Go talk to the TAs.* They might recommend better textbooks or prepare a "translated" handout.

☺ *Do a Web search.* You'll find that professors at some other schools put their class notes on the Web.

☺ Investigate the science encyclopedias at the library.

Studying from Class Notes

Why spend the energy taking nice, two-tone organized notes if you're never going to look at them again? The best time to look over notes is right after the class—to reenforce concepts. In lecture professors will occasionally cover material or give an example that is not in the textbook (a good clue to what he or she thinks is important). Use your notes! Look them over. Compile and process. Class lectures highlight the most important concepts of all the material.

Studying from Problem Sets

A problem set with an explanatory solution set is a gold mine. Homework sets serve to condense and summarize the class material (which has already refined the textbook material) down to the really important stuff. Read about the 80–20 Rule in the next chapter! That important 20 percent will make a debut in the problem sets before it makes an encore appearance on the test (and if it's really special it makes a comeback on the final). The point is this: Keep all homework solutions. Look over them when they are made available (don't bury them in a folder). See where you went wrong. Revel in where you were cleverly right. Notice better or alternative methods. Finally, if the TA or grader needs to readjust your homework grade, he or she will take more kindly to an immediate plea than to the end-of-the-term petition of I need two points somehow to get a B+.

LEARNING BY OSMOSIS

CHAPTER 8

Quizzes, Tests, and Exams

The only real differences between quizzes, tests, and exams are their percentage value of your entire grade and the frequency in which they are given. Quizzes are usually worth less than tests and may occur as often as once a week. A professor who prefers tests may have three or four in a term at "good stopping points" in the material. Exams, on the other hand, are the most comprehensive form of test and are usually given at the end of the course and sometimes during the middle of the term (midterms!). There will always be one professor who thinks the way to reduce class anxiety is to call the final exam "a quiz." However, the more frequently a professor tests you on the material, the more likely you are to learn it. In terms of the method for studying, all testing should be approached the same way. Of course, the best preparation for an exam is to stay on top of your course work during the whole quarter or semester, but this isn't always realistic or even possible. In the following sections, unless otherwise specified, "tests" will refer to any kind of testing.

STUDYING FOR TESTS

Top students often put less time into studying than the rest of us. Doesn't seem quite fair, does it? The difference isn't intellectual ability, it's their ability to organize efficiently and focus intently on the material they are studying. Anyone can do the same thing following these fabulous steps to better prepare for tests.

1. Organize.
2. Produce a game plan and study sheet.
3. Go over old tests.
4. Review class and text notes.
5. Practice problems.
6. *Know* your study sheet.

It looks like a lot of work, but it isn't really. You can attack the whole list at once or take a couple of steps at a time. Not all the steps will be weighted equally in importance or time; these factors depend on the class and type of test you are facing.

Step 1. Organize Your Troops (You and Your Notes)

You've gotten up early. You've primed yourself to hit the books . . . just bought a new highlighter, a waterproof felt-tip pen, and a decent stash of junk food to sneak into the library. You bike to the library, lock up, and secure a cubicle that looks knowledge inducing. *Then* you realize you've forgotten your exam outline—so to remember everything, take a quick look at the following checklist.

The Complete Don't-Leave-Home-without-Everything Checklist

☐ Class notes and handouts
☐ Subject study guide (if available)
☐ Highlighter
☐ Pencils
☐ Big eraser
☐ Scrap paper
☐ Class textbook and class pack (even if you never used them).

☐ All problem sets and solutions (and any from other years).
☐ Syllabus
☐ Test outline
☐ Calculator
☐ Extra lead or a pencil sharpener
☐ Sticky tabs (to mark important pages)
☐ Spare change for vending or photocopy machines

Wait! Before you head out the door (fully equipped) to study—if you need to spend some time getting organized, do it now while you are at home. Rearrange notes, homework sets, solutions, outlines, and any other loose items in an orderly form in your binder or folder. Now is also a good time to unearth

---

The Top 10 Reasons Why Engineering Tests Are Better than Liberal Arts Tests

1. No essay questions.
2. Your grade is determined by what you've learned rather than how well you can BS.
3. Grading is seldom subjective.
4. You get to draw pictures and use cool symbols.
5. Rarely will you be tested on readings.

6. A 65 percent can get curved up to a B+.
7. You are encouraged to use a pencil.
8. You don't have to outline engineering solutions before you start writing.
9. Some schools give more time for engineering exams.
10. You get to use your calculator.

notes you forgot you ever took (in a different notebook). Completing your notes and sorting the stack of information in a logical sequence before sitting down to study will save time and prevent a good deal of frustration.

Step 2. Be Strategic and Formulate a Game Plan

Tests are skirmishes! Exams are war! Studying for tests is a strategic exercise in preparation, especially when time is short (isn't it always?) and you have a sizable amount of material to cover. A good strategy considers three elements.

1. *How worthy is your opponent?* Size up the test. What are you in for? A rout or a walk in the park? In sizing up the test, you are anticipating how much time you should spend on and how deeply you should delve into each topic. Look back at old tests (first test tells all) and talk to upperclassmen. Some professors will devote a whole class to reviewing for an exam while others will just remind you of the date. Always be on the alert for any hints the professor or TA might give regarding the exam.

A note about review or study sessions. Always try to go to the first review session a professor or TA offers. You may find the sessions very useful or a waste of time. It is best to attend a study session after you have done at least a preliminary review of the material so that you have a better idea of your own questions and the relevance of your classmates' questions. It may turn out to be more beneficial to go to the professor's office hours or make an appointment with the TA instead of wasting precious last minutes.

Besides learning as much as you can about the structure and nature of the test, how else can you derive information? The table on the next page provides some key words that should alert you.

2. *Anticipate the attacks.* What will be on the test? Look at how your professor grouped the classroom material and predict what types of questions will be asked. Consider the type of questions you would ask if you were teaching the class. Here are some clues to what will show up on the test or exam:

☺ *What are the professor's favorite problems?* Think about any material or problems that really rocked his boat. Did your professor tell an anecdote or draw on the chalkboard—something he usually doesn't? Sometimes professors will even warn the class to "look out for this one, you'll see it again."

☺ *What kinds of problems integrate several concepts?* These problems are very popular with professors because they can test you on many things while asking only one question (or sometimes one question with eight parts).

Professors who make up their own homework problems (instead of assigning text problems) tend to have similar problems on their tests.

Key Word(s)	What It Means to You
Open book	• Get familiar with the textbook's index! Put labeled tabs on pages with important graphs or tables. Don't waste time during the exam flipping through the text! • This test won't be any easier than a closed-book test—if anything, harder. • Stick to studying concepts rather than details. Details are usually too much of a freebie. • When preparing for the test, spend less time memorizing and more time practicing problems. • Aim toward not even opening your book during the test. Often, you won't have the luxury of time to do so.
Closed book	• Use problem sets as an indication of which equations you should memorize. Professors will not usually expect you to have memorized random formulas on closed-book tests. • Look for tests from past years by the same professor. • Try to find out if any charts, tables, and so forth will be provided. This will give you an indication of whether problems that require those will be on the test. • Work as many text examples as possible. It's a *closed*-book test for a reason!
Equations provided	• Guess which equations will be provided and what kinds of problems and solutions incorporate those equations. Study those especially! • When preparing for the test, spend less time memorizing and more time practicing problems.
Crib sheet (a.k.a. cheat sheet)	• Don't forget to allot time to write out your crib sheet neatly. • To get the most on your sheet, user a copier to neatly (and legibly!) reduce notes and good problems. • Stick to studying concepts rather than details. Your crib sheet should cover the details. • When preparing for the test, you can spend less time memorizing and more time practicing problems.
Proofs	• Be prepared to spend some time memorizing. • Try to get your hands on as many examples as possible. Often a professor can give only a limited number of proofs.
Cumulative	• Focus most of your studying on the *last third* of the course. The most recent material is usually stressed the most because earlier material has been covered on previous tests. • When studying the earlier material, use old tests as a guide.
Take home	• Take home or take no prisoners means open books and notes (you can be tested on anything) and an open-ended amount of time (meaning it will take *much* longer than the regular test period to complete) within a specified period. • If you have an ample amount of time to complete the take-home test, you may simply want to organize and lightly

(continued)

	review the material before the test is given to you. Then delve into specific subjects once you have been given the test.
	• Well before the exam is given out, check out any helpful library books relating to the topic.
Multiple choice or fill in the blank	• If you think some vocabulary will turn up, be prepared to spend some time memorizing.
	• Look over boldface words in the textbook.
	• Know equations for quick plug and chug solutions.
	• Know the units and dimensions you are dealing with to eliminate obviously wrong choices.

☺ *What do the text and study guides deem important?* Look at applicable problems in Schuam's and the textbook. Common problems that might not make an appearance during class may occasionally show up on tests.

☺ *What do you not know well?* No kidding—it will probably be on the test. The material we often know the least about is the stuff taught right before the test.

3. *Make a list of likely targets and deploy your forces accordingly.* Formulate your game plan by listing concepts, laws, and methodologies on a single piece of paper. Label each concept with the means by which to master it. Were there particularly good problem examples from the book? Explanatory handouts from the class or TA's section? Class notes that clarified an important topic? Problem set solutions that spelled out a procedure? Your strategy for better learning the material shouldn't be simply to reread the text chapters you've covered in class. *The major part of the test will most likely cover specific concepts illustrated in problem sets.*

Deploy your forces accordingly by producing a sheet (or a limited number of sheets) that address your game plan and from which you will do most of your studying. Study sheets can include formulas, derivations, proofs, diagrams, definitions, steps to solve a problem, example problems, definitions, pertinent page references, and reminders to yourself.

Step 3. Review Old Campaigns (Tests)

Review both your own old tests and tests from previous semesters or quarters, if possible. Are there any additions you should make to your game plan and study sheet? Old tests are useful to you for two reasons.

1. *Old tests offer clues to the professor's testing style.* If you have old tests that are comprised of analytical problems only, you shouldn't spend much time memorizing definitions or theory.

2. *Old tests are a great resource for extra practice questions.* Tests from past courses may also include material you didn't realize was important.

☞ **The 80-20 Rule.** Twenty percent of the material in the course will account for 80 percent of the test problems and questions. This comes from an expansion on the Pareto Principle by Adam Robinson, cofounder of the *Princeton Review.* Pareto was a 19th-century Italian economist and sociologist who noted that from any group of objects, a small fraction contributes the most to the whole.

Step 4. Review Class and Text Notes

You should do most of your studying from your summary sheet, but reviewing notes will help you fit the theory and application puzzle pieces together for the big picture. Being able to understand and apply engineering theory will propel your knowledge from the short-term holding tank to long-term storage.

Class and text notes will reveal significant subjects or points that you might have missed earlier preparing your alpha[1] summary sheet. Add 'em on. You should now have a thorough estimation of the test material and how far along you are.

Step 5. Practice Problems

You don't prepare for a campaign by reading books; you practice what you think you will encounter out there on the battlefield. The bulk of your "study" time should be spent training. Work through drill problems. Look up references that explain the reasoning behind the method. Go through each section and make a list of all the problems you should practice. Pull problems from old tests, your study guide, or any homework sets for which you have solutions. Check off the problems as you work through them and make notes beside the ones that were particularly challenging or would make solid test questions. Work through the problems in a logical order and don't waste your time on problems without solutions!

Step 6. Know Your Study Sheet

When you cross off the final item on your game plan, it's time to learn your study sheet. Yes, this is boring, but after everything you've done, memorizing is a cinch! The best way to do this is to make yourself rewrite it from memory. It will take more than a few tries. An open-book test or an exam with equations included doesn't make you exempt from this step! A high recall speed during an exam will produce a sharper, more confident mind and allow for extra time at the end for checking over your work.

☞ **Should the all-nighter be an option?**
Turn to page 121 to find out!

---

[1]Before a product is released to the public, it often goes through many revisions. The first version of a large project (e.g., software) or part of a project (e.g., layout drawings for one part of a product) is often called the "alpha" version; likewise, the second version, after adjustments and corrections, is called "beta," and so on.

Ideally you want to be able to ace every test while accumulating omnipotent knowledge. In engineering, you can sometimes get away with getting pretty good grades when you don't really have a clue about what is going on. This is the studying shortcut version of the problem set shortcut (see page 68) and can be accomplished by memorizing steps or methods instead of learning the cause-and-effect relationships. Absolutely try *not* to do this; if you skate through the principles and material now, it *will* come back to haunt you.

On the flip side—if you are frustrated because you know every relationship and definition, and your tests don't reflect how well you really understand the material, then you need to concentrate more on general problem solving and less on the details.

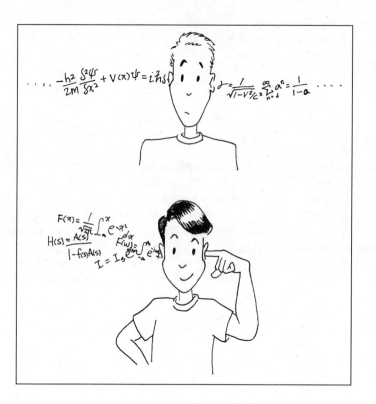

CHARGE! THE TEST

Keep in mind that the most important issue when taking *any* engineering test is time. So don't forget your watch! Some engineering professors take pride in testing your endurance and mental stability by delivering exams that require twice as much time and clarity than you are given. When heading into a test, remember:

The goal is to produce error-free work quickly and efficiently.

This takes practice, but not to worry—you will be given plenty! How do you start off?

When you get the exam:
- ☺ *Take a quick inventory.* Flip through it to identify the number of questions and estimate the amount of time you have for each. Also note the relative weight of the various problems.
- ☺ *Start with the easiest question and move to the hardest.* The idea is to complete the questions that you know and leave extra time at the end for the problems that will take you longer to figure out. Consider it stretching for the run.
- ☺ *Try not to leave the highest weight problems until the end.* This is the only time you probably should not leave the hardest problem to the end.

When tackling a problem:
- ☺ *Read* all *directions before jumping into solving the problem.* Engineering professors sometimes like to tack little short-answer questions onto the end of wordy problem statements.
- ☺ *Circle units.* That way you won't forget to check if they are consistent.
- ☺ *Draw a diagram for clarity whenever you can.*
- ☺ *Plug numbers into equations at the very end of your solution.* Doing this saves time and writing, and reduces chances of human and decimal point errors.
- ☺ *Carry the units through the equations to avoid conversion errors.* This is extra writing, but the units will be self-checking.
- ☺ *Never leave a question blank!* Even if you have absolutely no idea what it may be about, jot down some equations, laws, or definitions that you think are in the ballpark. See page 101 for help in reasoning through the tough ones.
- ☺ *Keep an eye on your equations and numbers while you are working through them.* If the equation doesn't look quite right, it probably isn't. Double-check as much as possible as you progress through the test in case there isn't time to go back and recheck answers.

WHAT'S THE MODE OF ATTACK?—MULTIPLE CHOICE, SHORT ANSWER, OR LONG ANSWER?

Multiple Choice

Tests with multiple-choice problems can be good for the test taker or conversely detrimental. Check out the following test question:

A quartz piezo-electric crystal with a thickness of 1.5mm and a voltage sensitivity of 0.055 $V \cdot m/N$ is subjected to 175 psi pressure. What is the voltage output?

(a) 99.5 V (b) 14.4 V (c) 0.144 V (d) 86.2 A

The good news: Multiple-choice questions give you the answer! Granted you may not know which of the above four answers is the correct one, but if you are having a hard time getting started, they will provide useful clues. The bad news: Professors sometimes don't give partial credit on multiple-choice tests.

To be a master at multiple choice:

☺ *Look for clues in the choices before you work the problem.* The answers provide possible clues on the units and ballpark value of your final answer.

☺ *Eliminate answers to improve your chances.* Occasionally one choice is a freebie elimination. How can an output voltage be in amps? Cross out (d).

☺ *Check those units.* Incorrect choices are often traps for those who forget to convert.

☺ *Work the problem only as far as needed to select the answer.* If you are taking a "scantron" (a test where you fill out the bubble sheets), don't spend time documenting your process if you won't get credit for it.

☺ *Don't stress if your answer is slightly off.* The solution below gets 99.8 V as the final answer—what gives? Round-off error can throw you off slightly. Here the error occured in the conversion from psi to N/m^2. Converting pressure to N/m^2, 175 psi = 1,205,750 N/m^2. This effects the final answer with $E = 99.47$ V.

A quartz piezo-electric crystal with a thickness of 1.5 mm and a voltage sensitivity of 0.055 (V·m/N) is subjected to 175 (psi) pressure. What is the voltage output?
→ convert to metric!

(a) 99.5 V   (b) 14.4 V   (c) 0.144 V   ~~(d) 86.2 A~~

$$E = gtp$$

$$t = 1.5mm = 0.0015m$$

$$g = .015\ V \cdot m/n$$

$$p = 175\ psi = (175\ lb/in^2)\left(\frac{6.895\ E3\ N/m^2}{lb/in^2}\right)$$

$$\approx 1.21\ E6\ N/m^2$$

$$= \left(.055\ \frac{V \cdot m}{N}\right)(.0015m)(1.21\ E\ 6\ N/m^2)$$

$$= 99.8\ V\ \rightarrow\ \boxed{a}$$

Short Answer

Short-answer engineering tests can take one of two forms: qualitative or quantitative. Either should be easy if you've learned the theory and memorized the right equations. A qualitative problem from an intro C Programming class might be:

What is the difference between $\&x$ and $*x$?

For quality answers, a one or two sentence answer with an example of each is the best way to go. Questions like this come directly out of assigned readings or class lecture. Your answer to the question above might read something like this:

& is an "Address-of" pointer operator. Given a particular lvalue, it returns the memory address in which the lvalue is stored.

* is a "value-pointed-to" pointer operator. This operator takes a value of any pointer type and returns the lvalue to which it points.

A quantitative chemistry problem might be:

What is the *pH* of a solution if $[H_3O^{+1}] = 7.83 \times 10^{-6}$?

Short-answer problems that require calculation define "plug and chug"; there isn't much to figure out, just use an equation. This problem simply checks to see if you know the equation: $pH = -\log[H_3O^{+1}]$. Your answer should look something like this:

$$pH = -\log [H_3O^{+1}]$$
$$= -\log [7.83\ E{-}6]$$
$$= -(-5.106)$$

$$\boxed{pH = 5.11}$$

Long Answer

Long-answer problems are the most notorious, the most frequent, and the most draining. Even when you do well, you can still feel like a stampede of elephants trampled over you.

> Physicsman is chasing Ann Tygravity when she appears to materialize on the roof of another building. He musters all his potential energy and takes a *horizontal* flying leap from the roof of his building to hers. Her building is on the other side of a busy street (20m) and 10m shorter. (a) What must be Physicsman's starting velocity to jump onto Ann Tygravity's rooftop? (Assume he needs 1m to land.) (b) How long will it take him to make the jump? (c) Will Ann Tygravity get away? (She needs 30s to get away.) (d) If Physicsman jumped at an angle 10° above the horizon with the same speed you calculated in (a), how far could he jump then? (e) Does he still land on the building (it is 10m wide)?

To make the long-answer problems less problematic:

- *Draw a diagram!* A simplified free body diagram or a flowchart illustrating related items will help tremendously.
- *Cross out parts of the problem that are unnecessary.* Physicsman may be everyone's hero, but he won't help you solve this problem.
- *Label the parts of your solution.* It becomes more obvious if you answered all parts of the problem.
- *Write down all equations you think apply.* It helps having all the equations you need in front of you.
- *Watch the clock.* Budget your time so you have time to attempt each problem.
- *Pull a stapled test apart.* Flipping through pages is an annoying way to take a test (also annoying for others to listen to). If a problem takes up more than one page, keep the first page next to you as you start on the following page. When you complete a problem, retire it to a separate "out" pile.
- *Cross out instead of erasing.* You may want to refer back to it.

Physicsman is chasing Ann Tygravity when she appears to materialize on the roof of another building. He musters all his potential energy and takes a *horizontal* flying leap from the roof of his building to hers. Her building is on the other side of a busy street (20m) and 10m shorter. (a) What must be Physicsman's starting velocity to jump onto Ann Tygravity's rooftop? (Assume he needs 1m to land.) (b) How long will it take him to make the jump? (c) Will Ann Tygravity get away? (She needs 30s to get away). (d) If Physicsman jumped at an angle 10° above the horizon with the same speed you calculated in (a), how far would he horizontally jump then? (e) Would he land on the building if it was 10m wide?

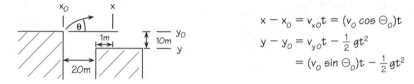

$$x - x_0 = v_{xo}t = (v_0 \cos \Theta_0)t$$
$$y - y_0 = v_{yo}t - \frac{1}{2} gt^2$$
$$= (v_0 \sin \Theta_0)t - \frac{1}{2} gt^2$$

(a) Horizontal jump: $\ominus = 0 \therefore v_{yo} = 0$

so vertical distance $\quad y - y_0 = -10m$

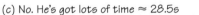

$$= (v_0 \sin \ominus_0)t - \frac{1}{2}gt^2$$

$$-10m = -\frac{1}{2}gt^2 \quad \rightarrow \quad t = \sqrt{\frac{(20m)}{g}}$$

horizontal distance jumped: $\quad x - x_0 = (v_0 \cos \ominus_0)t$

$$(20 + 1)m = v_0\sqrt{\frac{(20m)}{g}} \quad \rightarrow \quad v_0 = (21m)\sqrt{\frac{g}{(20m)}}$$

$$\boxed{v_0 = 14.7 \text{ m/s}}$$

(b) From (a): $\quad t = \sqrt{\frac{20m}{g}} \quad \rightarrow \quad \boxed{t = 1.43s}$

(c) No. He's got lots of time $\approx 28.5s$

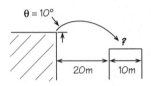

$\theta = 10°$

20m   10m

(d) $y - y_0 = -10m = (v_0 \sin 10°)t - \frac{1}{2}gt^2$

$$\frac{1}{2}gt^2 - v_0(\sin 10°)t - (10m) = 0$$

$$t = \frac{-b \pm \sqrt{b^2 - 4ac}}{2a} = \frac{2.55 \pm \sqrt{2.55^2 - 4(4.91)(-10)}}{2(4.91)} = \boxed{1.71s} \enspace -1.192s$$

$$x - x_0 = (v_0 \cos 10°)t = (14.7m/s) \cos 10° (1.71s)$$

$$\boxed{x - x_0 = 24.8m}$$

(e) YES! $(x - x_0 < 30m)$

Four Things to Consider if Your Answer Seems Way Off

1. Check your units.

Did you forget to convert? Did you remember to account for prefixes like giga or milli? Does the answer seem wrong when it isn't because the test question uses English units when the class examples and homework problems with which you are familiar use SI units?

2. Recheck any numbers you took from a chart, table, or graph.

It is *very* easy to misread values on those cramped charts and tables. A minute interpretation difference of a log-log or semi-log chart can produce a monumental difference in the final result.

3. Could the answer actually be correct?

Maybe it would look more realistic if you converted mols back to kmols (1000 mols = 1 kmols). Or perhaps your professor is using an extreme situation for a "more interesting" problem.

4. Write a note to maximize partial credit.

If you are out of time and the answer violates "engineering intuition," make a note along these lines: "The answer appears to be off, but I don't have time to find it. A more reasonable answer might be . . . "

Haven't a Clue. . .

You've hit a question and you have *no idea* where your professor dug it up. The hardest questions on the exam are often not as awful as they appear—if you can decipher the question and make the connection to the material. Tough problems are frequently some application of important theory that was not covered specifically in a class example. Something somewhere applies!

OK, the most important thing to remember when you have no clue:

Never EVER leave a question blank!

If you leave a question blank, you are telling the professor that you don't know anything . . . which is always untrue. So write down an equation, a definition, or some sort of reasoning that shows that you do know something about the concept. For a 15-point problem, 2 or 3 points is always better than zero points.

Just because you have no earthly idea how to do a problem on the first pass doesn't mean the solution won't come to you while you are working on other problems. Sometimes all you need is a warm-up problem to get you thinking or another question that might trigger the remembrance of an equation or method that had previously eluded you.

OK, now you have completed the whole test except for the hardest problem. Now what? Here are few tips that will help you put up a fight:

1. *What are the variables involved?* Rewrite them and get rid of some of that blank space on your test paper. It is easier to take an inventory when unknowns, constants, and knowns are listed. What equations and/or methods that you covered employ these numbers or variables?
2. *Look for key words in the question.* Wording or terminology can often point you in the right direction. Even if you don't hit the correct answer, you'll probably get points for being in the right ballpark.
3. *What has the professor* not *covered with the other questions?* Use the process of elimination. Reason through the test and think about what else is likely to be on the test, but isn't.
4. *Is there a key chart, graph, or table that may fill a void in the information?* Double-check whether any charts are included with the exam or if the professor has written any notes on the board.
5. *Just start writing.* Actively tackling the problem can trigger your memory of a method or a similar example. Should you run out of time, you'll at least have work down on the paper.

6. *Are there any common elements with a similar or related problem?* Does this problem sound sort of like another problem you studied? Writing down a general formula might jog your memory to other uses.

7. *Examine the units for clues.* What quantities are you working with and how might they be related? For example:

MPa (1 MPa = 1 megapascal = 10^6 pascals = $10^6\ N/m^2$ = 1 N/mm^2)

could be stress or pressure and they are both equal to force divided by area which is equal to mass times gravity divided by length squared.

8. *Rewrite the problem in your own words.* You may learn things you didn't pick up when reading through the question. This will also ensure that you understand exactly what is being asked.

9. *If you really get stumped at one part, use poetic license to fill in the blanks.* State in your own words that you are not sure how to complete the problem given, but with a sign change or given a particular variable, you are able to work the problem and produce the following result. Of course, your solution is incorrect, but most of your method will be correct. You probably just forgot an integral or simple equation and will only lose minor points.

10. *Could you maybe derive an equation you've forgotten?* In part (c) of the sample Physics problem, you could have more efficiently used $x - x_0 = (v_0^2/g)\sin 2\Theta$ instead of working through the equations of parts (a) and (b). Our test taker, in fact, derived it by working through the solution the "long way."

Worse comes to worst. If you have a test or exam that is just absolutely and utterly horrendous—due a miscalculation on the professor's part, certainly not because you didn't study—take comfort in that *it is a horrendous exam for everyone* and it will soon be over. Imagine this test as a take-home exam and you had three days of it instead of an hour or two.

GETTING THE TEST BACK

Whether you were victorious or suffered a humiliating defeat, don't forget to look over the professor's comments and place the test somewhere retrievable (i.e., not the recycled paper bin) for final exam time.

If you think there may be a grading error, take your test home and work the problem again—and then make an appointment with your professor. If you used a different (but correct) method to solve a problem, take the reference notes or textbook with you to your meeting. Professors are bombarded with students claiming they have been unjustly wronged; your tact and conscientiousness in handling the situation will likely gain you their respect.

When the Going Gets Tough . . . Dealing with Ruts and Unmarked Pitfalls

The man who makes no mistakes does not usually make anything.
English proverb, 19th century

Every college student in every major passes through an academic or emotional rut at some point. Engineers seem to fall into more than their share, not because we are uncoordinated (well. . . a few maybe), but because we *care more*. Engineering students (and maybe a few premeds) tend to be more concerned about their grades, what they are learning, how much they are remembering, and how all the theories fit into the Big Picture. Add to that, they already know that engineering isn't easy and the more retained the better off they'll be.

When floundering in the middle of a rough week, it can be perplexing to imagine that college is supposed to be fun. At the end of the quarter or semester when you look back at the work you have managed to complete, you see that it *is* worth it. And that doesn't even compare to the glee you feel when picking up your diploma after years of omnipresent problem sets, programs, and projects.

There are three central things to keep in mind when the ground takes on a negative slope:

1. *Balance.* Have other active interests besides school (TV doesn't count).
2. *Take care of yourself.* Try to get a reasonable amount of sleep.
3. *Keep at it.* Playing Graham Nash's "Chippin' Away" in the background helps.

Ignore your classmate with the megaphone voice who can be (easily) overheard trumpeting that all his classes are so easy. Either he:
A. is on drugs.
B. spent more time on the last problem set than the entire class combined and is feeling a little insecure.
C. got solutions from an upperclassman and will bomb the exam.

105

106

CHAPTER 9
When the Going
Gets Tough . . .
Dealing with Ruts
and Unmarked
Pitfalls

You can pretty much count on the fact that if you are having a tough time coping with the workload, grades, knowledge assimilation, and life, your classmates are, too. Some pitfalls or ruts can be minimized or avoided altogether; others unfortunately cannot.

Next is a quick overview of the biggies and some possible solutions.

RUTS

Burnout

Burnout comes in many forms but is most often characterized by a lack of motivation. Additional symptoms can include academic disinterest, exhaustion, sleepiness, and procrastination like never before. Burnout can result from overdoing it the previous quarter, taking a required class you aren't interested in, a bad professor, too many nonacademic commitments and demands, or frustrating work arrangements (teams for math homework?!).

Burnout Solutions

☺ *Chose classes wisely.* If the semester looks like it might be intense, try to take a fun elective. If you can't take a free elective, try to pick an engineering elective that offers something different from the other classes. For example, if it looks like all your classes will be lecture and problem sets, try to take a lab.

☺ *After your freshman year, try to take hard or work-intensive classes first semester or over the summer.* The first semester or quarter after summer you usually return to school ready to hit the books; the second semester or second and third quarters you return to school wondering where the vacation time went. Summer school may be taught at an accelerated rate, but the atmosphere is often more laid back because everyone takes fewer units.

☺ *Reward yourself for a job well done.* Take an afternoon off or go buy a new CD.

☺ *Find a compatible person you study well with.* Your study mate doesn't even have to be an engineer.

> ☞ **Study groups aren't always successful.** The "more the merrier" and more merriment can mean less work is accomplished.

☺ *Maintain other interests.*
☺ *Take study breaks* (See page 109).
☺ *Change your regular study routine.* Try studying in a new place: the library or a different study room. Buy some earplugs and head for a coffee shop or try to listen to music while studying.

Sleeping All the Time

107

CHAPTER 9
When the Going
Gets Tough . . .
Dealing with Ruts
and Unmarked
Pitfalls

Caffeine just doesn't work anymore? Napping may not be so bad if it allows you to work at odd hours when you are most productive. Problems arise if you need more than one nap a day or if you are always tired and unproductive.

Solutions to Your Need for Naps

☺ *Break the cycle.* Go cold turkey and go to bed at a decent hour.
☺ *Change your eating habits.*
☺ *Set regular hours for yourself and stick to them.* Tell friends the latest time they can call you (then turn off the phone because they will still call). You will be more productive and time-efficient with your schoolwork when you have a bedtime.
☺ *Don't nap to procrastinate.* We fool ourselves out of work.
☺ *Exercise more.*

Too Much to Do

Napping? Who has time for napping? Even if you could nap—which you can't because you can't sleep, because you're not sure if napping is a luxury you should allow yourself, and anyway you would dream of engine cycles playing like film loops—but you *can't* because there are still a million things to do. Whew!

Solutions to Help Slow Down

☺ *Don't look too far ahead.* Keep your immediate goals and assignments in the forefront of your mind and keep end-of-semester projects in the background.
☺ *Remember that anxiety is a wasted emotion.*
☺ *Cut down on your caffeine consumption.* People who consume too much caffeine tend to be running a million miles an hour without focus or completion of anything. Read more about caffeine and kicking the habit starting on page 116.
☺ *Are you multifunctional?* Then organize notes and punch holes in handouts while you are on the phone, take a book to the gym to read on the stationary bike, or review solution sheets while waiting for an appointment.
☺ *Reevaluate how you spend your time.* If you think there isn't any more you could possibly do, accept that you are doing the best you can and be proud of yourself.
☺ *Keep things in perspective.* Bad grades suck, but things could be much worse.
☺ *Talk to peers who seem well adjusted and happy.* How do they do it?
☺ *Keep your batteries charged and motor running.* Chapter 10 looks at the physical and psychological symptoms of stress and anxiety and how to deal with it (see page 119).

CHAPTER 9
When the Going
Gets Tough . . .
Dealing with Ruts
and Unmarked
Pitfalls

TV and the Wednesday Night Beer

Television is bubble-gum for the mind.
FRANK LLOYD WRIGHT
American architect (1867–1959)

This pitfall also could be called "Getting Sucked into Things You Really Don't Have Time For." Procrastination is one of those things that when it rains, it pours; it is difficult to procrastinate only a little bit. One beer turns into three or four, and a half hour of prime-time TV turns into three hours. Procrastination can make an assignment that should require two hours to complete into one that takes the whole night.

Solutions to Beat Procrastination

☺ *Tape shows.* Tape just the shows you want and watch them later at a study break or when you have time. That way you can fast-forward through commercials, too!

☺ *Set and meet targets.* There is always some work you could be doing with engineering, so there never really is a time when you can get your "work done early and go out." Give yourself a target goal (like finishing all the problem sets due for the next two days and start on the one due Friday), so you can occasionally go out during the week and watch the full prime-time marathon if you want. Slack-off nights, when you can afford them, will keep you from getting burned out.

☺ *Go to the library, coffee house, study lounge, or picnic table on the lawn.* Social studying is better than not even looking at a book. Getting out of the house gets you away from phone calls, bad-influence roommates, and other distractions.

☺ *Have productive study breaks.* The key to a good study break is feeling sufficiently refreshed to tackle the books again. Try to set a time limit for your study break and then reevaluate how you feel. It's OK to extend your break *if necessary*, but it shouldn't be more than double the time you originally allotted.

109

CHAPTER 9
When the Going
Gets Tough . . .
Dealing with Ruts
and Unmarked
Pitfalls

The best study breaks are those that offer:

☺ A change of environment like a trip to the athletic center or cooking a real dinner (not from a box). Walking from your desk to the soda machine in the basement usually won't do it.

☺ A jog down memory lane such as writing a letter or calling a friend from home.

☺ Increased adrenalin like playing intramurals or finding a date for a weekend party.

☺ A glimpse of life off-campus like watching the news, volunteering as an after-school tutor or mentor, or going to the store.

☺ A change of mental scenery like flipping through a magazine or reading a chapter from a good book.

PITFALLS

Computer Hell

Aaghhhhhhhhhh! The server went down. Disk quota exceeded. Error of type 15. System crash and you forgot to save. It's not supposed to do this!! There really isn't anything you can say to comfort someone who just lost a valuable file or program. What makes computer disasters even more frustrating is that they usually can be avoided.

How Not to Let Your System Crash

☺ *Start all computer assignments early.* There are always bugs and better ways.

☺ *Save often.* Be paranoid.

☺ *Revisit computer lab hours.* Plan accordingly.

☺ *Backup.* Have backups of all programs, operating system disks, and installation disks for your own computer.

☺ *Always have one extra print cartridge and pack of paper.* You always run out 10 minutes before the deadline.

☺ *Know someone whose system is compatible with yours.* This is important in case your computer and printer aren't communicating properly and you need to get your assignment in.

110

Chapter 9
When the Going
Gets Tough . . .
Dealing with Ruts
and Unmarked
Pitfalls

☺ *Buy lots of disks and a portable plastic disk carrier.* You can never have too many disks. Leave several disks in the box in your backpack.

⚠ **Protect your disks!** If you don't have a transporter box, use a ziplock or an envelope. Funky things happen in backpacks.

☺ *(Actually) label your disks.* So you know what is on the disk and someone else knows who to return it to.
☺ *Invest in surge protectors.* Double-check that they are computer grade and don't forget to protect peripherals too!

Can't Get into a Class You Need to Get into?

This can be particularly frustrating. If you have a legitimate reason why you should be in the class, go talk to the professor. It might be a wild-goose chase, but if you are polite and *persistent* you will always get in. At some schools, professors will ask hopeful students to fill out a registration form with a question like "What do you hope to gain by taking ChemE 103?" Write a lot! Go all out! This little essay may determine whether or not you get into the class.

End-of-the-Term Slam

111

CHAPTER 9
When the Going
Gets Tough . . .
Dealing with Ruts
and Unmarked
Pitfalls

Dead Week (a.k.a. Study Week) is a week at the end of the semester or quarter when professors are not allowed to teach new material or assign additional homework because students should be devoting their time and energy to preparing for finals. No one has yet figured out why most schools don't have a Dead Week for engineers. Of all students, engineers could really use one. We're the ones dying!

Whoa! The workload is *increasing.* You're not imagining it. The professor probably realized he was a bit behind in the class schedule and material. You'll hopefully have read the assigned readings and have kept up so that your lack of time and abundance of stress won't be quadrupled in an attempt to have a strong end of the term.

Surviving the Slam Solutions

- ☺ *Keep a running list of assignments to complete and things to do.* You should give emphasis to priority items and how much time you can spend on each.
- ☺ *Put your social life on hold.* Don't feel bad about returning low-priority phone calls until exams are over.
- ☺ *Prepare in advance.* Buy study foods, highlighters, paper, a nice pen, and so on. Do your laundry so you'll have clean clothes. It all helps to get yourself into a work mode.
- ☺ *Eat easy-to-fix meals.* If you can't afford to grab quick bites at the school cafeteria, keep lasagna in the freezer and sandwich stuff in the fridge.

Adverse Advisors

Advisors are most often moonlighting professors. When you consider everything an average professor is expected to do, it's not so hard to understand why advising undergrads usually falls pretty low on their list of priorities. Often, the difference between a good advisor and a bad advisor is timing. But, if it seems like your timing is consistently bad, here is some advising advice:

- ☺ *Be your own advisor.* Read the course manual and your curriculum sheet thoroughly. If you have questions, talk to a well-liked professor in your department.
- ☺ *Talk to upperclassmen.* Find out about good classes to fullfill requirements. Ask for recommendations for good upper-level classes that match your interests.
- ☺ *Call the registrar's office for university policy questions.* How are transfer credits handled? Are students in your major allowed to take classes as pass/fail? Often the university registrar knows the policies better than department advisors.
- ☺ *Need a signature?* If you need something signed and your advisor continues to break appointments with you, contact the departmental secretary and explain the situation. Secretaries, used to dealing with that particular professor, are usually very helpful.

CHAPTER 9
When the Going
Gets Tough . . .
Dealing with Ruts
and Unmarked
Pitfalls

Can't Stand the Instructor

Napoleon complex? Ego just too big for the room? Clearly more interested in research than teaching? Try not to let it get to you. Consider it practice in dealing with all the frustrating people you will encounter in life. It is not a good idea to take an individual complaint about a professor (or advisor) to a dean or department chair because rarely (and sadly) do students have any input into the tenuring of professors. Complaining will only make *you* look like a bad seed.

Poor Professor Solutions

- ☺ *Deal.* Don't take it personally.
- ☺ *Switch sections.* Find a different professor and give as your reason: "time conflict."
- ☺ *Do the best you can.* Why make it worse by not learning anything?
- ☺ *Try to work with the TA instead of the professor.* This applies to homework help.
- ☺ *Is it the professor or the course? Consider this:* Is it the professor you really dislike or the material he or she is teaching? If it is the material, check whether there is a substitute course. If it is the professor, try not to hold it against the material.

Girlfriends, Boyfriends, and Other Possibly Neglected Distractions

If they are not in engineering, they probably won't understand why you spend much more time with your books and calculator than with them. Just hope they have a life apart from waiting for you.

CHAPTER 10

Balancing It All

We came, we saw, we kicked some ass.
—San Francisco Radio Station Slogan
Based on Julius Caesar's (100–44 B.C.)
much uttered *Veni, Vidi, Vici*
[I came, I saw, I conquered]

There are two campaigns we must win while passing through our years of engineering education. The first, a balancing act—*life, school and sanity*—must be maintained, and the second—*the Ben Balance* (as in Ben Franklin)—must be achieved. The sooner we are aware of our need of balance and the sooner we are able to achieve and maintain it, the less stressed and more knowledgeable we become. It is possible to have a fulfilling social life while still excelling in our classes.

LIFE, SCHOOL, AND SANITY

It takes most engineering students one to two years to find their life, school and sanity (LSS) balance. Freshman engineering students usually take one of three routes:

1. You overwork, overstudy, don't get out much, but get grades of which you can be proud. (No life, school, borderline sanity will cross over to the dark side your sophomore year.)
2. You absorb college life to the fullest by going to every football game, keg, and Greek row party, but college is tougher than high school and your grades reflect this. (Life, no school, sanity is questionable.)
3. You have a social life, pretty good grades, and enough stress that implosion is a very real possibility. (Life, school, far from sanity)

Catching on? The goal of course is to have and maintain a balance of all three if you weren't lucky enough to be born with the quality of adaptable equilibrium. This isn't to say that life, school, and sanity are all equal. They aren't and they shouldn't be. Picture three glasses of water (of various sizes if you like) on a tray. You are trying to carry the tray with the glasses through an obstacle course without spilling a drop. Keep the tray balanced and you will spill none.

Don't take years to find your LSS balance—start now! Each of us has our own system of organizing ourselves, so a balancing act for one person may or may not apply to another. Think! A good starting place is to consider a time in your life when everything seemed to be going *perfectly*. What were you doing that made things run smoothly? Here are more ideas to get you started on finding your LSS balance:

☺ *Stay healthy!* Read the next section!
☺ *Fight ruts.* A bad rut can mean no life, no school, and no sanity. See Chapter 9 for strategies to pull yourself out of the most common ruts.
☺ *Give yourself a break.* Beating yourself up for a bad grade does no good. Use the negative energy for extra studying, a four-mile run, or something else productive. Doing poorly on a test can occur even when you know the material inside out. It's just the nature of engineering tests.
☺ *Get organized.* Know what is due when. Keep track of assignments, meetings, and social events. Choose your personal assistant: lists, notebook, day planner, sticky notes on the bulletin board, wall calendar, or Palm Pilot.
☺ *Get involved!* No matter how much time you think you don't have, everyone has time for at least one extracurricular activity. A real college education is about experiencing everything that interests you. Involvement with diverse school clubs and organizations also ensures that you have a good balance of friends outside of engineering.

KEEPING YOUR BATTERY CHARGED AND MOTOR RUNNING . . .

> *Plentus venter non studet libenter*
> *(A full belly does not study willingly)*
> —Latin Proverb

The easiest way to keep your LSS balance is to stay healthy. You've undoubtedly heard it before. Freshman orientation week tends to include a barrage of information on the dangers of drinking, lack of sleep, and the importance of nutrition and exercise. Let's look at the biggies that most affect engineers.

Caffeine: Engineer's Friend or Foe?

It's 10:00 P.M., you have a final exam the next morning. You are exhausted after having two exams already today. You estimate that you have a minimum of four hours of studying to do before you feel like it's worth even showing up at the exam. You need to wake up and start studying. What's the natural

tendency? Plug in the coffee machine. Put a six-pack of soda in the freezer for rapid cool. Hunt down some of those stay-awake pills. Is that a good idea? Probably not.

Know the caffeinated facts:

1. *Caffeine can stress you out.* Caffeine is a stimulant that mimics the effects of adrenaline, the principal neurotransmitter of a stress response. In moderate amounts (50–300mg), caffeine acts as a mild stimulant by increasing the heart rate and blood pressure. Excessive amounts (> 400mg) can cause anxiety, insomnia, headaches, jitters, nausea, and even irregular heart beats.

Where Those mg Come From[*]

Coffee (5 fluid oz.)	mg.
Drip (auto)	137
Drip (nonauto)	124
Percolated (auto)	117
Percolated (nonauto)	108
Instant	60
Decaffeinated	3

Tea (5 fluid oz.)	mg.
Imported	54
U.S. brand	46
Oolong	40
Green	31
Instant	28
Decaf	~1

(All applicable brewed for 5 min.)

Soda (12 fluid oz.)	mg.
Mountain Dew	54
Coke	45
Pepsi	38
RC	36
7-Up, Sprite	0
Fresca	0
Hines Root Beer	0

Chocolate	mg.
Baking chocolate (1 oz.)	25
Sweet dark chocolate (1 oz.)	20
Milk chocolate (1 oz.)	6
Chocolate milk (8 fl. oz.)	5
Hot chocolate (6 fl. oz.)	5

Nonprescription drugs (standard dose)	mg.
Alertness tablets	200
Diuretics	167
PMS relief pills	60
Cold/allergy medicine	22–36
(Some) pain relief pills	20

*Where the data in this table comes from: For nonprescription drugs: Labels. Everything else: Pennington JAT, Church HN: *Bowes and Church's Food Values of Portions Commonly Used*, 14 ed. (Philadelphia: Lippincott, 1995) through the fab Healthy Devil Web site at Duke University.

2. *Caffeine is a diuretic.* Let's leave it at that.
3. *Caffeine is a drug.* Regular caffeine drinkers or users can suffer withdrawal symptoms (even if they miss one day!), which may include headaches, irritability, and mild depression.
4. The rest of it probably ain't so good for you either . . .
   - *Carbonated drinks* are high in phosphorus which depletes calcium in your bones.
   - *Tea and coffee* contain tannin which, when consumed within an hour before to an hour after mealtime, significantly reduces iron absorption.
   - *Diet sodas* have aspar-what? The jury is still out on aspartame, the sugar substitute in diet sodas. There has been much debate on possible health risks. The Center for Science in the Public Interest recommends that "if you consume more than a couple of servings a day, consider cutting back. And to be on the safe side, don't give aspartame to infants."
5. *There are ways to kick the habit!* Switch to decaf. Try herbal teas (they're caffeine free). Try mixing half decaf with half regular. Read labels. Those who have kicked the caffeine habit say they that their study habits have improved because they can focus better.

Is It Possible to Spend Too Much Time with Your Computer?

You wouldn't think so. As an engineer, however, the postcomputer marathon feeling is familiar: stiff shoulders, strained eyes, sluggish fingers, and a dull ache in the lower back. When sitting for a long period of time studying or hacking, one all-important thing you should do that is guaranteed to improve your cranky mood and muscles considerably is:

Take a 15-minute break every two hours (or less).

Stretch. Walk around. Harass your roommate. Splash cold water on your face. Just move! What else can you do? Keep reading.

Watch Your Eyes!

Problems have been associated with too much time looking at a computer monitor. Farsighted users may experience blurred vision and discomfort and those with astigmatism may experience eye soreness and headaches if looking at a display for an extended period of time.

To fight eye fatigue:
- Clean your screen regularly.
- Maintain a high contrast between the text and the background. No green on red!
- Try not to work in the dark. Your roommate won't mind the desk lamp.
- Adjust your screen to your viewing pleasure. When you are working, the top should be slightly below eye level and the screen should be 18 to 28 inches away.

Are you a CAD jockey? Do you engage in debates that extol the virtues of the three-buttoned mouse? Do you brag about how many lines of code you can write in a night (whereas another major might brag how many pages he or she can turn out in a night)? In the past decade, repetitive motion disorders have increased alarmingly with many of them attributed to the computer. The National Institute of Occupational Health determined that eight or nine repetitive movements in a minute did not provide adequate time for the wrist to produce enough lubrication for its narrow passageway of ligament and bone (the carpal tunnel).

To stay out of the carpal tunnel:

- Move your whole arm instead of just your wrist when doing mouse work.
- Keep a loose relaxed grip on the mouse. A clenched grip means you should probably take a break anyway.
- When typing, keep your shoulders relaxed with your upper arms and forearms at a right angle.

How can you lower your desktop? Most desks have a large pencil drawer above the opening for your legs. Try pulling it out and moving your keyboard into it with some books to help adjust the height.

Sit Smart (at Home)

After reading Chapter 6, you know how to sit smart in class, but what about at home? Some companies actually have lunchtime seminars on how to sit "correctly." The ideal chair for long hours of sitting at a desk is one that is adjustable and provides firm, comfortable support. Doesn't sound much like the standard-issue dorm desk chair, eh?

How to prep your chair to work with you:

- Do a quick upholstery job: Put a bed pillow on the seat!
- Adjust the floor with the college edition dictionary and thesaurus so that your feet rest flat.
- Check out the back of the chair, too. Add another pillow, if necessary, to make sure it supports your lower back.

Anxiety and Stress

College students feel the pressures of anxiety and stress not only in class, but also in regular day-to-day life. Both are brought on by transition and change. The average college student moves six to eight times in four years. That's not much time to settle into a routine. Reentry students may not be moving as often, but they feel the stress of trying to balance their family and/or job with classes.

Anxiety

Anxiety is the apprehension you feel in response to a real or perceived threat. Reactions are brought on by a sense of distress or through the use of drugs, such as cocaine, caffeine, alcohol, and amphetamines, that affect the nervous system. Reactions can range from mild uneasiness to intense panic. You may have heard someone say that they had an anxiety attack during an exam and simply couldn't function. It can be a frightening experience.

Physical signs. Dry mouth, flushing of face and neck, nausea, lightheadedness, hyperventilation, increased heartbeat, sweating, tremors, and muscle tension.

Psychological signs. Apprehension, difficulty sleeping, restlessness, irritability, fear, panic, impatience, lack of concentration.

Stress

Stress is the response of your body when your internal balance is disrupted (by positive, negative, unusual, or even normal events) and your system must readjust. Stress is a very common aspect of everyday life and can be beneficial in situations such as taking an exam or driving in a snowstorm where heightened alertness is desirable. Stress becomes a problem when it exceeds a productive level and interferes with your ability to work effectively. Unmanaged high levels of stress can cause physical deterioration and illness after a period of time.

Physical signs. Chronic fatigue; change in appetite; increased use of drugs, alcohol, or nicotine; aches and pains for no reason; change in sleeping patterns.

Psychological signs. Irritability, changed behavior, difficulty focusing.

Prevention Is Key

- *Exercise, and eat well.* Mom was right. Exercise and eating well increase your energy level. Twenty minutes of exercise three times a week. Three balanced meals a day.

⚠ **What you consume (or don't consume) can affect your memory.** Everyone handles stress differently. During exam week you may forget to eat or you may eat too much. Maybe you celebrate one exam down with a drink down the hatch. Rediscover the food pyramid from junior high health class! Preliminary research has shown that crash dieting or overeating can negatively affect how much you learn and retain. Additionally, frequent or heavy binge drinking has been linked to the death of brain cells. Don't waste your tuition!

- *Get sleep!* The average person needs eight hours. Aim for six hours (at least). Getting enough sleep allows your mind to unwind (psychologists believe that dreams can be an outlet for anxious and stressful feelings) and your body to repair itself. Tasks that require thinking (e.g., homework) can take much longer than usual if you are sleep deprived

because it is much harder to focus. It not only matters how much you sleep, but when you sleep. Consecutive sleeping allows you to cycle through all the necessary sleep stages so that you feel rested.

The All-Nighter
Sometimes It Is Unavoidable . . . but Try to Avoid It!

Two things work against you when you pull an all-nighter. The first is that when you are tired, your body has difficulty focusing on the material you are attempting to learn. Not only will it take longer for you to remember, but you may not even remember the information very well. Your second obstacle is that you are "cramming"; you are attempting to learn by studying for long uninterrupted intervals. Psychologists call this "massed practice" and have found that it is much less effective than "distributed practice" where you spread the studying out over many days or weeks.

- *Find ways to relax.* What works for you? Classical music in a dark room? A warm tub and a good book? A quiet half hour checking out the evening view from a hilltop? A morning jog before classes?
- *Hang out with people who give off good vibes.*
- *Ask for help when you need it.* And *don't* be embarrassed about it. All schools have a counseling center that offers advice on stress management techniques like muscle relaxation and meditation. They also can provide professional help on an individual level.

School clubs and organizations are cheap, fun, mind-expanding (in the best way), and offer a good change from the schoolbooks. Engineering students tend to steer clear of getting "too involved" on campus because they don't think they have the time. True, you don't have the time other majors have, but don't sell yourself short! Many students find they complete the same amount of schoolwork whether they have several outside commitments or few. With less to do, engineers take more time to complete assignments than is necessary. It's a form of Parkinson's Law (with some literary license)—Work expands to fill the time allotted.

Usually at the start of every school year there is a campus organizations fair on one of the school's big green lawns. You don't have to be a freshman to ask freshman questions and try something new. Organizations and clubs are a great opportunity to dabble in the areas that interest you.

- ☺ *Try to do most of your sampling your freshman year.* The first year you have a bit more time and you won't be tied down with too many responsibilities. As your schoolwork intensifies with (sophomore and junior) years, you should pick your favorite activities and stick with them.
- ☺ *Look into popular campus activities even if they might not be your cup of tea.* There are reasons why they are popular.
- ☺ *Involvement doesn't have to conflict with study time.* Go on an alternative spring break program (students who do community service) or, after your freshman year, become a freshmen orientation leader.
- ☺ *Excuse yourself, with apologies, from (minor) events.* These can interfere with work or are just seemingly pointless.
- ☺ *Involvement produces good leaders.*

THE LIFE OF AN ENGINEERING STUDENT— WORK HARD, PLAY HARD

Alas! Something has to give to do everything, right? Well, it depends on how you define *everything*. Engineers don't have the freedom (like some Econ or History double majors we know) to spontaneously decide to have margaritas, play glow-in-the-dark frisbee golf, and then serenade the early morning shoppers at the convenience store across the street from campus. But then, *that* sort of activity can be saved for Christmas break with your high school friends. However, since a few hours of focused work can crank out a problem set, tell your friends that you are skipping the preparty, but you'll meet them later. You may have to give up some of the fun, but not all.

- ☺ *Be fashionably late to parties.* You can study longer (especially if your roommates go out) and you don't usually miss anything anyway.
- ☺ *Don't feel like a nerd for staying in on a weekend night to get some work done.* In on Saturday night can be a good trade for an outing on Thursday night.
- ☺ *Do blow off your work every once in a blue moon.* How often do blue moons come? This is OK for special occasions.

☺ *Think before you drink.* If you don't get any work done with a hangover, then don't get blasted Saturday night if you plan on cramming all day Sunday for a test at 9:00 A.M. Monday.

☺ *Plan ahead for weekend events.* Don't miss the road trip to Mardi Gras or Graceland to do work, unless you really have to. Get as much completed as you can before you leave. Don't take your books with you. Have a good time. Those memories last longer than a mediocre grade on a Ceramics quiz.

PLAYING A VARSITY SPORT OR WORKING WHILE IN SCHOOL

Playing a varsity sport while in school full time is very much like holding down a part-time job. And whether you work 5 hours or 20 hours a week, it can be stressful to find time to do everything you would like. If you are an engineer committing more than 10 hours a week to a sport or job, free time and social activities will become a rare luxury. The difficulties are more than not having enough time to study and to complete assignments; there also are time conflicts such as work or training schedules that conflict with laboratory classes, review sessions, and TA and professor office hours. Students who are able to successfully balance school with a sport or work usually do so in one of two ways:

1. From the beginning of their freshman year, they successfully integrate sports or jobs into their school schedule.
2. After getting a good grounding freshman year and advice from busy upper-classmen, they allot time successfully for school and work commitments.

The above scenarios are completely different in that folks who fall in category 1 might have to work or play a sport to afford to attend school and live, whereas in category 2 the student may have more financial flexibility. If you even think there may be potential conflicts with your schedule and class office hours or review sessions, talk to your TA and professor. They will probably make special arrangements with you and be much more willing to help by E-mail.

If you are interested in finding a job for a bit of cash or work-study (financial aid may require it) while in school, picking the right one could give you some good engineering experience and allow you to study on the job.

Job Prospects for Engineering Majors

Below is a short list of suggested jobs:

1. Work for a professor in your department.

Busy work, medium schedule flexibility (might be able to swing time off during exams).

Unfortunately, undergrads working for professors do a lot of grunt work like cleaning samples, filing and cataloging articles, and helping grad students with data collection. However, the benefits far outweigh any of the mindless work: You get good hands-on experience in a research environment that may

even turn into a real research position as an upperclassman; you become acquainted on a personal level with the professor, grad students, and other folks around the department; it looks good on your resume; and frequently you are granted time off during exams. Working in your department is also a good choice if you think you may be heading to graduate school because you will get some exposure to a research environment. If you are interested in working for a particular professor, contact him or her directly. If you aren't sure, keep your eyes and ears open; sometimes small job openings are posted on bulletin boards or in the departmental E-mail. If not, contact the department administrator.

2. Computer monitor.

Sometimes very busy, sometimes dead, medium schedule flexibility (often expected to work through exams).

Working at the Help Desk forces you to learn more about computers. This is always an asset to the engineer. Some computer labs are very social while others are tense.

3. Bartender, cocktail server, runner at a *nice* restaurant or happening bar.

Very busy, little flexibility (unless you can trade shifts, but restaurant/bar managers can grow impatient with students).

So why would you take a restaurant or bar job? Jobs like this pay cash for just a few hours of work if you pick an upscale restaurant or bar. Food runners and cocktail servers are known for being able to work a four- or five-hour shift and pick up ~$100. The downside is that you will probably have to give up a weekend night, the income is not guaranteed, and restaurants and bars don't take Christmas and spring breaks.

4. Engineering internship.

Real work, flexibility varies.

Internships provide incredible insight into and experience in engineering as a profession. They can give you direction and an education that cannot be gained by taking classes. The good news is that internships often pay very well, but the drawback is that a good internship can be difficult to balance while attending school full time.

5. Checking ID cards or working the Reserve Desk at a quiet library.

Not usually busy, medium schedule flexibility (usually have to work during exams).

Good for studying, relaxingly calm (but tedious?).

6. An outside interest job.

Busy, but fun; variable flexibility.

Tevas with wool socks? If you are the hiking, outdoorsy type, see if the rec center has a job in its outdoor education department. Why not get paid for what you might be doing in your spare time? Some of the best-paying, flexible jobs can be found by checking the school newspaper want-ads. Often the psychology

department is looking for human guinea pigs at $25 dollars an hour to fill out questionnaires (sometimes worse). You might also see excellent short-term, paying jobs for engineering students needed to test web sites or work on textbook solutions manuals.

THE BEN BALANCE

Ben! The same legendary Mr. Franklin exulted in U.S. history textbooks, legendary for the key-on-the-kite-during-lightning picture: inventor, printer, writer, politician, diplomat, and scientist. He was a colonial American Renaissance man with only two years of formal education under his belt. Had he gone to a modern-day engineering school, he might not have come out so well rounded.

Part of the problem is *how* many engineering schools (and thus engineering students) tend to view the nontech classes. The few liberal arts classes an engineering student needs to take are often seen as a *requirement*. And while both Anatomy and Technical Writing may be requirements for a biomed engineering student, Anatomy isn't usually regarded with the same disdain as Tech Writing. Of course, you may be more interested in Anatomy, but Technical Writing is a vital part of the engineering picture, too.

Why do we hear people remark that "engineers must be smart, but gee— they lack common sense!" Wait! That's not right. Engineers are supposed to be the most logical of the homo sapiens, although . . . well, often their logic is discrete on the infinitesimal scale, and they sometimes miss the macroscopic. Engineering education can sometimes be too one-sided, left-brain heavy. A better balanced brain makes for a better problem-solving engineer and a more knowledgeable person.

Where might engineers need some right-brain remedial? How about in the realm of culture and nonscientific current events? They are interested, but they are mostly up to their eyeballs in work and extracurricular commitments. You've heard that education isn't solely in the classroom. That's true, and it's up to you to fill in the gaps and grow like yogurt under a heater. Your engineering classes can't do everything.

So what do you do? Think critically about yourself. Picture the type of person you want to be when you graduate. Pinpoint areas where you think you are lacking and find a fun way to tackle them.

Look Where You Are Lacking and Fill in the Gaps!

Art.

Does the word *art* make you uncomfortable? Do you cringe at the thought of having to draw a self-portrait? Not only is art distantly related to engineering (*technes*, the root of technology, is Greek for "art"!), but it is a necessary tool (the root *pencillis* of pencil is Latin for "brush"!) for the engineer. Think how often you have to draw diagrams when solving problems. Decent drawing skills are necessary for the practicing engineer to communicate exactly what they are working on. Getting a little art in your life doesn't mean you have to sign up for a theater or art class—although that would definitely make you a Renaissance person.

Do the following to revive and utilize your latent artistic talents:

☺ *If your school has an art library, go poke your head in.* If you think *you* are uncomfortable in an *art* library, try to get an art major to go to the engineering library.

☺ *Notice the random art exhibits in the student union.*

☺ *Keep a design log.* Engineers involved in design wouldn't live without them. What products peeve you? Is it a pain to adjust your rear-view mirror accurately? If you were a design engineer, how would you redesign it? Sketch your ideas and add explanatory notes. Interesting articles and tidbits also can be taped or jotted down in logs. Famous inventions are born in design logs.

☺ *Read the plaques on the campus statues.* Try to figure out the material and method used to produce the artwork. How is it manufactured?

☺ *Go to school plays and concerts.* Especially if you have a friend participating.

☞ **Get the most out of your school!** Go to traveling art exhibits, free speakers, web page or cooking workshops, goofy dorm field trips, sporting events, cheap movies, theater productions, fly-fishing classes at the rec center, photography or bartending classes at the student center. It's inexpensive, fun, and a good break from your regular schedule.

Out of Touch

Your parents called to ask if everything was okay after they saw on the news that three tornados had touched down within 100 miles of your school. Tornados? It rained a lot and . . . hey, now that I think of it, there were a lot of branches on the ground . . . It's easy to lose yourself in your work and miss the boat on current events. The worst part is that the full realization that you have no idea what is going on becomes painfully obvious when you try to keep up a conversation with your newly acquired significant other's father or a professor you would like to impress. The microcosm syndrome can leave you feeling clueless and self-absorbed. Having an idea about what is going on off campus will give you a better grounding and more chances to challenge your own ideas and beliefs.

Be omniscient!

☺ *Pick up a newspaper with your morning soda.* Even the comics are a start (you have to glance at the headlines to get there).

☺ *Listen to AM talk-radio during your shower or the commute.*

☺ *Get involved with a community service group.* The hardest thing about doing community service is taking that first step to get involved. After that, it's easy, fun, and the rewards come back to you tenfold.

☺ *Find on offbeat coffee house or bookstore.* These sometimes have newspapers from around the world. The fewer people you recognize from school, the better.

☞ **If your university is in or near a decent-sized city, get out and explore!** Seek out local favorites on your own and by asking around. Check the student union and admissions/orientation office for touristy pamphlets and maps. If you aren't in a major city, check the map and find a friend with a car . . . it's time for a road trip! A weekend or even an overnight road trip to a ballgame, the beach, or Montreal will inject some fun into a dull semester.

☺ *Seek out extracurricular activities that involve dialogue with others.* This could inspire you to think about your own values. Good examples for contacts are environmental organizations, political action groups, and committees that organize campus speaking events.

Life 101

Do you feel left out of political discussions? Do interest rates (and the big deal over them) leave you baffled? You should pick up a myriad of useful life tools before you graduate to make you a better engineer and world citizen, like:

☺ *Intro classes in social sciences and humanities.* These are great for a crash course in the human race. Everyone should definitely have an Introductory Economics class to learn all the stuffy terminology and understand annual reports. Other good nonrequired intro classes for engineers are Psychology, Accounting, Public Speaking[1], and English Composition.

☺ *Workshops sponsored by your dorm, student government, student center, or career center.* Such workshops can teach you the ins and outs of buying (and repairing) a car, how to find the right life/car/fire/accident insurance, and explain basic mortgages and investments. Workshops and seminars are usually quick and useful.

☺ *Opportunity.* Just dive in!

The Big Picture

So you are learning all this useful, tangible knowledge about the interaction of complicated scientific and computational systems. But how much do you really know about the relation of humans to the technology that engineers generate? Well, let's see . . . engineering ethics might have popped up your freshman or sophomore year in an intro engineering class, but often that's it! Engineering has a colorful history filled with eccentric and fabulously odd people, but unless you read the unassigned historical section in the first chapter of a course text, you miss out. Most texts don't include the interesting things anyway. Did you know that the young Isaac Newton carved his name on almost every school bench he occupied? Or that Ada Byron Lovelace, the first computer programmer, was an incorrigible gambler? It's also useful to know how engineering reaches into other realms like law, medicine, philosophy, and sociology.

---

[1]Some engineering schools will not give humanities/social sciences credit for public speaking. Check with your advisor to see where it figures into your degree requirements and electives.

☺ *Good classes.* History of Science or History of Technology, Engineering (or Science) Law, Technology and Public Policy, Management of Technology, Technology and Society.

☺ *Go to campus forums on "Science &* (Pick one): Ethics, Religion, Third-World Countries, Society, Science Fiction."

☺ *Audit a class for a day.* Granted, having the time would be a luxury, but if a friend's law or engineering class is having a professor come to speak about applying for a patent—and that sounds interesting to you—don't be bashful. Chances are the professor won't even notice your presence and, if he or she does, they would probably be flattered.

☺ *Do an engineering co-op.* Co-ops are internships for which you get school credit, often with a required paper or sometimes a weekly discussion group. Co-ops allow you to see how engineering and your skills fit into industry. Also, you can earn good money.

☺ *Field trips!* Take advantage of field trips sponsored by engineering societies. Plant tours are the most common destination. Industry field trips may give you some insight into where you may (or may not) want to work.

Hands-On Application

Are you an ME who feels lost when you look under the hood of a car? Have you had a circuits class, but wouldn't know a capacitor from a resistor unless someone drew their symbols? You are certainly not alone. One of the complaints heard most often about engineering education is that there is not enough application of taught theory. Part of the reason for this is that many of the professors who are teaching you to become a practicing engineer have *never* practiced engineering "in the trenches" themselves. Wild, eh? Some professors took the academic route of getting a bunch of degrees and then taking a teaching post at a university. So, don't be surprised if you feel you are not getting enough hands-on experience.

Tips about how to get handy.

☺ *Take the offered machine shop class.* Even if you are a biomedical engineer, it is still useful to be able to produce your own prototype with your own hands.

☺ *Load up on lab classes.*

☺ *Read scholarly and popular journals. Scientific American, Discovery,* or any magazine published by an engineering society would be excellent choices.

☺ *Look into classes at nearby technical schools.* Vocational and technical schools offer great classes in Surveying, Auto Mechanics, Welding, Electronics, and other useful skills. Take these during the summer break when you have more time.

☺ *Keep your eyes and ears open for on-campus workshops.* Especially workshops that teach crash courses on UNIX or how to use multimedia equipment.

☺ *Plan your own fun field trip.* How about going to an air show or hands-on science museum?

☺ *Get involved with society competitions.* Solar Car Project, Concrete Canoe Race, Aerial Robotics Competition, Autonomous Ground Competition, Aerodesign Competition, just to name a few.

Communication Skills

Communication skills are what many practicing engineers wish they had mastered while they were in school. On-the-job engineers find themselves giving presentations to their co-workers and superiors, writing letters and memos, and constantly interacting with folks of various backgrounds who may or may not have technical know-how. Good communication skills can be acquired quite easily, but you may have to take your own first step because many curricula place no emphasis on it.

Communicate with this:

☺ *(Useful) Communication classes.* Any one (or more!) of the following classes: Public Speaking, (easy) English, Technical Writing, Technology Management, and so forth.
☺ *Book clubs and discussion groups.* Check with the university bookstore or library.
☺ *Check out or purchase a vocabulary book.* Some are actually kind of informative—know what *callipygian*[2] means? Big words make you look witty and clever.
☺ *Work for the school newspaper or literary/humor magazine.*
☺ *Any extracurricular group that requires verbal idea exchanges.*

Other People

Nope. Not kidding. You needn't look forward to the vacation at home to be around "normal people." As awesome as we engineers are, we do get on our own nerves. Part of having a good balance for ourselves is having a good balance of diverse friends.

More Friends, More Fun: Places to Look

☺ Community or public service (on campus or off).
☺ Theme dorms (like French or Philosophy).
☺ Intramurals and off-campus athletic leagues.
☺ Greek organizations.
☺ Religious groups.
☺ Common-interest clubs like photography or hiking.

THE COUNTER-CREATIVITY MYTH

You may have noticed how people who place themselves on the science/math end of the spectrum tend to make disclaimers for their art ability, correctness in spelling, and creativity in thinking. Engineers (and not just students) make many disclaimers.

---

[2]Having a shapely buttocks.

It brings to mind the reported classroom research about singing, dancing, and drawing told by Adam Werbach (who at age 23 was elected president of the Sierra Club, an American nonprofit environmental and public interest organization). As he tells it, a small group of researchers with clipboards in hand visited a kindergarten class. The first question they asked was:

"How many of you can sing?"

The kindergartners (somewhat shyly) all raised their hands; they had just sung "Puff the Magic Dragon."

The researchers then asked, "Well, how many of you can dance?" There were some smiles and all the students raised their hands.

"Good, then how many of you can draw?" the researchers asked. All the giggling children raised their hands.

The same researchers visited a senior-level class at a university in upstate New York. Again they asked questions.

"How many of you can sing?" The college students looked blankly at the three researchers. A lone hand timidly raised in the rear of the auditorium.

"Uh-huh, and how many would say that they could dance?" There were some smiles, but no one raised a hand.

Lastly, the researchers again asked: "How many people can draw?" A mere six or seven hands went up.

Hmm . . . What happened?

Some of the most famous scientists and engineers devoted a great deal of time to singing, dancing, and drawing and would you have guessed also weaving, poetry, and other fun things?

And there are many more who shatter the Counter-Creativity Myth. *Engineers are inherently creative because they are problem solvers.* Just think of McGyver. So, with the Ben Balance and LSS Balance you will never emit a disclaimer.

Who?	How We Would Know Them	Mystery Talent(s)
Sir Humphrey Davy	Rubbed two blocks of ice together on a subzero day and watched them melt to study thermodynamics and heat transfer	Poet
Albert Einstein	Theory of relativity ($E=mc^2$)	Musician
Galileo Galilei	Greatly improved the telescope, introduced Strength of Materials and Kinematics	Poet
Robert Goddard	Goddard Space Flight Center in Maryland, work in rocketry, invention of the bazooka	Science fiction writer
Sir William Rowan Hamilton	Law of multiplication of quadrions: $ij = k, jk = i, ki = j, ik = -j, kj = -i, ji = -k, i^2 = j^2 = k^2 = 1$ (used in vector analysis)	Poet
Fredrich August Kekulé	Kekulé structures: graph representation of chemical compounds with abbreviations of elements and dashes	Architecture
Johannes Kepler	The three laws of planetary motion	Artist, musician
Ernst Mach	Mach number describing a moving object's speed in air (Mach 1 equals the speed of sound)	Musician
James Maxwell	Maxwell's equations (one of which is Faraday's law) describing electric and magnetic phenomena	Poet, photographer
Siméon-Denis Poisson	Poisson's ratio relating lateral and transverse deformation in a material	Fiction writer
Charles Richet	Developed the first immune serum	Poet, playwright, nonfiction writer
Erwin Schödinger	Schödinger wave equation	Weaver

Dear Sir,

The fact that I beat a drum has nothing to do with the fact that I do theoretical physics. Theoretical physics is a human endeavor, one of the higher developments of human beings—and this perpetual desire to prove that people who do it are human by showing that they do other things that a few other human beings do (like playing the bongo drums) is insulting to me.

I'm human enough to tell you to go to hell.

—RICHARD FEYNMAN

American physicist, poet, artist, musician, and safecracker (1918–1988), in response to a request from a Swedish encyclopedia publisher for a copy of the photograph of Feynman (in shirtsleeves gleefully pounding a bongo drum) that adorned each volume of The Feynman Lectures on Physics. The publisher wished to "give a human approach to the difficult matter that theoretical physics represents."

Beyond the Bachelor's Degree—Things to Think About Midway Through

By the time you are a junior, you should have a general idea of what you want to do after you finish your bachelor's degree. The good news is that even if you don't and you are a senior, engineers tend to have more options than almost any other major (just look around at a career fair). Your analytically trained mind, tech-n-*abilities*, and computer-hacking skills will be a bonus when wandering through the job market.

So why do you have to start thinking about all this now? Because life after college comes up awfully fast when you are a senior. Interviewing for jobs will start in the fall of your senior year. Many graduate school and scholarship applications are due by January, and while you might not have a problem writing essays last minute and then express mailing them out, getting references from professors always takes a few days. But even before all that, you are forced to consider what you do want to do after you graduate and where you want to do it.

These days graduating engineers can do pretty much anything they want. Philosophy majors can't do a master's in Electrical Engineering, but electrical engineers can go to business school or law school (and hang out with the philosophy majors). Engineers are fully versatile! With that in mind, these are the three general routes a graduating engineer takes:

1. Become a practicing engineer! (This is the obvious one.)
2. Head to graduate school.
3. Take a route that's not-quite engineering. You use your skills in another area.

A LICENSE TO ENGINEER?

Before you get out a map to determine which route to take, consider this: No matter which career direction you choose to take—If you live in the U.S., take the Fundamentals of Engineering (FE) exam your senior year (or earlier if you'd like).

134

Chapter 11
Beyond the Bachelor's
Degree—Things
to Think About
Midway Through

The FE examination (it may be called the EIT or Engineering in Training exam depending on the state you live in), is the first step in becoming an officially licensed engineer. The rules governing licensure vary from state to state, but the process is fairly consistent. It is an eight-hour state board exam that you will take in some random school cafeteria or gymnasium if you aren't lucky enough to have your school host a site. After you have passed the EIT and have worked a few years under a PE certified engineer, you can apply to take the PE (Professional Engineer) exam that is specific to your discipline. With PE certification you get to put the cool initials, PE, after your name when you sign documents or letters.

The EIT is usually offered twice a year. Depending on your state, you may need to have graduated from an ABET-certified university or college (turn to page 46 for more info) to be eligible. Since most students take the exam their senior year, you should start looking into the registration process and all that good stuff by the end of your junior year.

The EIT (a.k.a. FE) Rundown: How the Process Works

1. Find your school announcement bulletin board with informational packets about becoming a certified engineer. If you have no idea where this might be, call the engineering dean's office and ask the secretary.
2. Grab a packet. Read it. Call or see your advisor if you have any questions. For additional information, you can also look at the National Society of Professional Engineers (**www.nspe.org**) or the National Council of Examiners for Engineering and Surveying (**www.ncees.org**) web sites.
3. Fill out all necessary postcards, forms, and so forth, and write a check for the application fee.
4. Mail it!
5. Sign up and attend an EIT prep course (often offered by your school) *if* you think you may need it. If your school doesn't offer a prep course, the NSPE has information on test preparation. If you would rather study on your own, look for the book *Engineer-in-Training/Fundamentals of Engineering Review: A Complete Review for the FE/EIT*, edited by Merle C. Potter.
6. You will receive a packet in the mail with the site of your exam, a formula and table booklet that will be the same as the one you will be given at the test, and some other information.
7. Take the test.

The Examination Itself

The EIT or FE exam is an *eight*-hour (in case you missed that earlier), multiple-choice exam divided into two four-hour sessions with a one-hour break for lunch. The morning session is a general exam (common to all disciplines) with 120 questions worth one point each. Questions cover all kinds of topics:[1] Mathematics (20 percent), Electrical Circuits (10 percent), Statics (10 percent), Chemistry (9 percent), Thermodynamics (9 percent), Dynamics (8 percent),

---

[1]The figures represent the percentage for each topic on the 1996 exams.

135

CHAPTER 11
Beyond the Bachelor's
Degree—Things
to Think About
Midway Through

Mechanics of Materials (7 percent), Fluid Mechanics (7 percent), Materials Science/Structure of Matter (7 percent), Computers (5 percent), Engineering Economics (4 percent), and Ethics (4 percent). You can see that mainstream disciplines have an advantage over narrower disciplines, however nearly all majors cover enough of this material to pass the exam. Following are some typical questions you can expect on the morning test.

Some might-be's on the morning exam:

6. The paraboloid 2 units high is formed by rotating $x^2 = y$ about the y-axis. Its volume is:
    (A) 2π
    (B) 4π
    (C) 6π
    (D) 8π

23. Consider the following program segment:

```
x = 2
y = 0
z = -1
for i = 0 to 2
(   x = x + 1
    y = x - y
    z = z*y
)
```

What are the final values for x, y, z?
    (A) $3, -3, 3$
    (B) $5, 2, -3$
    (C) $5, 4, -4$
    (D) $4, 1, -1$

49. In a series RLC network the applied voltage is $v(t) = 56.3\sin(144t)$ and the circuit current is $i(t) = 4.7\sin(144t + 0.27)$. The power delivered to the network at $t = 3 \times 10^{-3}$ seconds is:
    (A) 71.5 W
    (B) 84.2 W
    (C) 94.7 W
    (D) 140.4 W

73. An isobaric process is one with
    (A) constant volume
    (B) constant pressure
    (C) constant volume
    (D) zero heat transfer

110. Flow through a large river is to be scaled for a movie. The river has an average depth of 4m and a flow rate of 95 m³/s. The pump used for modeling the river has the capability of a 0.75m³/s flow rate. What depth should the movie river be scaled to?
    (A) 0.032m
    (B) 0.048m
    (C) 0.47m
    (D) 0.80m

(Answers, in case you were curious: 6. A; 23. D; 49. A; 73. B; 110. D)

136

CHAPTER 11
Beyond the Bachelor's
Degree—Things
to Think About
Midway Through

The afternoon session for the EIT or FE is offered in five disciplines (chemical, civil, electrical, industrial, or mechanical) and one nonspecific general exam. All exams are similar in format with 60 problems worth two points each. While the afternoon problems require more work than the morning problems, they tend to be grouped so that one answer leads to the next problem, or many problems use the same diagram. Although past scores on the discipline-specific exams have been slightly higher, many students still opt to take the general exam because they are already studying a broad range of problems for the morning session.

Afternoon problems that might make an appearance:

Given a set of equations represented by $[a_{ij}][x_j] = [y_i]$:
$$3x_1 - 1x_2 = 11$$
$$x_1 + 3x_2 = 17$$

1. What is the adjunct matrix $[a_{ij}]^+$?

(A) $\begin{bmatrix} 1 & 3 \\ 3 & -1 \end{bmatrix}$

(B) $\begin{bmatrix} 3 & 1 \\ -1 & 3 \end{bmatrix}$

(C) $\begin{bmatrix} 3 & -1 \\ 1 & -3 \end{bmatrix}$

(D) $\begin{bmatrix} -3 & 1 \\ 1 & 3 \end{bmatrix}$

2. What is the inverse matrix $[a_{ij}]^{-1}$?

(A) $\begin{bmatrix} -3 & 1 \\ 1 & 3 \end{bmatrix}$

(B) $\dfrac{1}{6}\begin{bmatrix} -1 & 3 \\ 3 & 1 \end{bmatrix}$

(C) $\dfrac{1}{9}\begin{bmatrix} 3 & -1 \\ 1 & -3 \end{bmatrix}$

(D) $\dfrac{1}{10}\begin{bmatrix} 3 & 1 \\ -1 & 3 \end{bmatrix}$

3. When using Cramer's rule, x_1 can be found by evaluating a determinant $|b_{ij}|$ and then dividing by the determinant $|a_{ij}|$. What is $|b_{ij}|$ for x_1?
   (A) 16
   (B) 17
   (C) 33
   (D) 50

4. What are the eigenvalues or characteristic values of the matrix $[a_{ij}]$?
   (A) 1, 2
   (B) 1, 3
   (C) 2, 4
   (D) 3, 3

Consider the following network:

137

CHAPTER 11
Beyond the Bachelor's
Degree—Things
to Think About
Midway Through

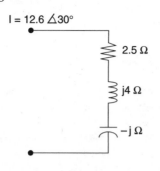

I = 12.6 △30°

2.5 Ω

j4 Ω

−j Ω

34. What is the average real power delivered to this network?
   (A) 64 W
   (B) 112 W
   (C) 198 W
   (D) 256 W

35. What is the apparent or complex power delivered to this network?
   (A) 138 VA
   (B) 309 VA
   (C) 452 VA
   (D) 703 VA

36. What is the power factor for this network?
   (A) 0.54
   (B) 0.64
   (C) 0.66
   (D) 0.78

(Answers: 1. B; 2. D; 3. D; 4. C; 34. C; 35. B; 36. B)

It doesn't look too terrible, does it? Too many engineering students do not take the EIT, some because they didn't know they should and others somehow justified skipping out. Take it! You have nothing to lose (failing it is the same as not taking it at all). Your EIT certification is the government's recognition that *you are an engineer*. Even if you are heading to business school, take it! You may change your mind about corporate life. And who wants to go back and study for an engineering exam that tests on four years of education (some of which you never even saw)? Still uncertain? Turn the page to see *No Lame Excuses about Taking the EIT Exam!*

After putting this final test behind you, you can put your education to the test.

ON TO BIGGER AND BETTER . . . THINGS? PLACES? ADVENTURES?

Where are you heading? What are you going to do with rest of your life? Where will you live? How will you pay your loans off? Whether you take a summer internship, a job, or apply for more education, you are going to need a resume (see *The Quick Guide to an Engineering Resume* in the box on page 138).

Check out a sample resume in Appendix E. Now you are ready!

1. *It costs too much.* Ouch! It does cost a little over the non-fun allowance quota. Gotta think of it as the gift that keeps giving.
2. *Don't have time to study.* It's your senior year! Projects are due! Job interviews! You haven't made one review session anyway. People have been known to pass with a good memory and minimal (no) studying. Don't forget a formula book is given to you for the exam.
3. *Don't need it to be a good engineer.* You're right in theory, *but* legally only a licensed engineer can offer services directly to the public. Especially if you are a civil or environmental engineer, with a PE, you will also be a higher-paid, faster-promoted engineer who can prepare, sign, seal, and submit plans and drawings to a public authority for approval.
4. *Eight hours of a weekend is too much to give up at the end of your senior year.* It *is* too much, so either take it in the fall before senioritis sets in or just take it at the end of the year anyway. It makes it easy to justify going out for a beer after reliving your engineering education compressed into eight hours.

The Quick Guide to an Engineering Resume

Gosh, there are many different resume formats you could *employ* to find *employment*. Check with your university or college career center to determine its recommended format. The format below is standard and is recommended for engineers.

Some Rules:

1. Use one side of one page.
2. Margins should be no less than ¾ inch on the right- and left-hand sides and ½ inch at the top and bottom of the page. This allows sufficient buffer space for photocopying and binding (for resume books).
3. Try to stick to white paper. Gray and beige paper do not reproduce as well as white.
4. For maximum clarity, use a font no smaller than 10 points.
5. It's better to be simple than slick.

The Breakdown

1. *Identifying information.*
   Include your name, permanent and school addresses, e-mail address, home page URL, and phone number with area code.
2. *Job objective.*
   Make a brief statement about the kind of position you are looking for. Your objective statement will alert the employer to your specialty, interests, and the internal department or division to which to forward your resume. Some good examples:
   - A civil engineering position, especially in environmental planning or geotechnical engineering. (CE)
   - A research position in computational mathematics preferably in close proximity to an apple tree. (Isaac Newton)
   - A position in digital design or signal processing. (EE)
   A side note: in some situations you may want to make your resume as broad as possible, and having a job objective can be restrictive.
3. *Education.*
   List your school(s), major, degree to be received (B.S., B.E., A.B., etc), projected graduation date, and dates of attendance. Schools should be listed in backward chronological order with most recent at the top. Summer school at home, community college, and overseas programs also can be included.
4. *Experience.*
   Experience can be any paid or unpaid jobs or duties that illustrate your excellent leadership, interpersonal, communication, and technical skills. Experiences also should be listed with

Continued

the most recent first. Include dates of employment, job title, employer name and location, and responsibilities and accomplishments. Start descriptive sentences with an action-oriented verb and highlight activities that would most interest your employer.

5. *Honors/Awards.*
   List honor societies, awards, scholarships, and distinctions in order of importance. Tailor the order of importance to the reader.

6. *Additional information.*
   This is the place for any other relevant or pertinent information such as languages skills, professional societies, computer literacy (list software), certifications, and outside interests.

The Engineering Job

Senior year becomes an exercise of a different kind of equilibrium: keeping up with school, arranging interviews (and possibly being flown to them), and outings with friends. An early jump on the job search process can leave you with valued free time and sanity once the schoolwork kicks into high gear. The following things will help you get your first engineering job:

☺ *Having had summer engineering internships.* Summer internships serve multiple purposes. They look great on resumes, help you make decisions about your future (did you like what you did?), and can lead to jobs after you graduate.

☺ *Having taken a co-op or an industry-sponsored class.* A co-op works much like an internship except you get school credit. Industry-sponsored classes are often upper-level design or research-type classes where outside companies or agencies contribute time, money, and possibly facilities for students to work on "real" projects. Strong performance during a co-op or on an industry-sponsored school project often results in a job or internship offer. Employers often look for students who have co-op experience because they believe them to be more committed and mature in their approach to work.

☺ *Use of your university's career center.* The center will lead you through the maze of resume production, interview strategies, networking, kiss-up cover letters, job fairs, and job searches. It's often a good idea to start attending workshops your junior year so you aren't slammed at the start of your senior year.

☺ *Keeping your ears open at the department.* Local companies and alums looking to fill jobs or recruit candidates often call professors.

☺ *Use of family and friends connections.* Nearly 80 percent of jobs are landed through connections. Something to think about!

☺ *Keeping it all in perspective.* Don't stress about making a "big life decision." Most college graduates switch from their first job to another within the first three years.

☺ *Having strong verbal and written communication skills.* Well-developed oral and writing skills are becoming almost as important as strong technical

140

Chapter 11
*Beyond the Bachelor's
Degree—Things
to Think About
Midway Through*

abilities. No matter how you cut it, engineers need to be able to communicate effectively and clearly regarding what they are working on and the proposed solutions. Second-round interviewers are even known to ask students to give impromptu presentations ("That's funny—the overhead projector worked this morning, would you mind going ahead without . . . ") during interviews.

☺ *Creating an interesting, professional home page.* Hopefully you will have a home page by the time you are a senior. If you don't, don't worry. HTML (Hyper Text Markup Language) is easy with the aid of a tutorial book or a campus workshop. When interviewing season arrives, it is usually best not to have a picture of your significant other on your web page. Better things to put on it are information and pictures of projects you've worked on and a downloadable resume.

The Inside Scoop on the Engineering Interview

Your technical competency (GPA) got you the interview, but now you need to get more than your foot in the door. Because the others selected for the interview also have the stamp of technical competence, you have two goals:

Make an impact and stand out from the crowd.

Just like you try to anticipate what a professor is going to throw on a test, you should prepare yourself for an interview by predicting not just the questions but how to respond in a way that makes the interviewer want to offer you a job on the spot.

Five questions that are frequently asked of engineering students include:

1. "So what do you know about us?"

Be prepared for your interview! Even if you think you know a ton about the company with which you are interviewing, check out its web site, do a magazine or journal search for current articles and issues, run over to the business library to look up statistics on the industry, and talk to professors. Keep a list of questions you would like to ask your interviewer (see question 5). It might pull time away from other work, but you'll forget all that when you get your job offer.

2. "Please draw a free body diagram of a femur bone."

You may be a good student, but how good of an engineer are you? Besides how well you know to respond to the problem, the interviewer may be evaluating you on two other qualities. The first evaluation may be how you handle having to perform in a stressful situation. The occasional interviewer has even been known to mislead you to see if you have enough confidence to stick to your own knowledge. The second test is to test if you can clearly communicate your ideas and problem-solving process to another engineer. The good news is that technical questions asked in interviews tend to be fairly easy (sophomore level).

3. "So I see here that you . . . "

Some interviewers will barely look you in the eye, and just go straight down your resume and ask you questions about past honors, jobs, and skills.

To stand out, have a "beacon" or two on your resume to ensure that you will be asked about it. A beacon is something that jumps out because it has an interesting name or may seem out of place (chair of the "Digital Art in a Digital Age" exhibit) , but shows that you are extremely well-rounded, multitalented, and adaptive to many environments ("You spent a semester in Chile?"). An interview means open season on your resume, so be prepared to talk in depth about anything on there.

141

CHAPTER 11
Beyond the Bachelor's
Degree—Things
to Think About
Midway Through

4. "You've described a positive quality, now please describe a negative quality about yourself."

This can be a tough question if you don't see it coming. Why would you tell an interviewer exactly what you don't want them to know? The interviewer is attempting to get an idea of the type of person you are. What are your values? What are you like to work with? A short succinct answer is the way to go, but the key to this question is to turn the "negative" quality about yourself into an asset for the company: "My mind never leaves work. I am always thinking about new ways to solve problems."

5. "That's it. Do you have any questions I can answer?"

Yes! Make an attempt to interact with your interviewer on a more individual level (How long has she been working at the company? What is his/her background?). Use this opportunity to show additional knowledge about the field ("I just started reading the book, *The Prize*. Have you read it? It gives such interesting insight on the history of the oil industry."). Reiterate your enthusiasm for the company.

Not to scare you, but some sadistic interviewers do try to rattle you, maybe by delving beyond casual conversation into a technical project you worked on, or by asking you to spit out a short computer code on the spot that reverses a text string. Maybe they are checking performance under pressure? Be prepared! Some interviews are love fests while others are weenie (you) roasts.

Little Things That Can Make a Big Impact on Your Job Interview

- ☺ *Come stocked.* In addition to your resume, bring a pencil, blank paper, and photographs and summaries of significant engineering work you have done. See the next point for what you do with your pencil and blank paper.
- ☺ *Give a planned-spontaneous presentation.* Draw an explanatory (well-practiced) sketch or diagram of a project you have worked on. The interviewer(s) will almost certainly ask about past projects. Make note before you go into your interview of what information you want your interviewer to pull from your responses. Your interviewer will be impressed with your ability to easily communicate technical concepts.
- ☺ *Lead parts of the discussion.* Think of the interview as a discussion with one of your Dad's technology-loving friends, not an an interviewer-interviewee conversation. Don't babble or feel you need to fill silences. Ask questions.
- ☺ *Use tech-specific lingo.* But use it correctly, don't overkill, and avoid acronyms the interviewer isn't familiar with! (Quadruple negative

142

*CHAPTER 11
Beyond the Bachelor's
Degree—Things
to Think About
Midway Through*

points.) Engineers have been hired on the spot for mentioning technical buzzwords or discussing specific trends in the area of expertise of the interviewer.

Don't Forget to Write a Thank-You Note

Sending a thank-you note to every interviewer you encounter is a good idea and shows professionalism (seems ironic—you get tortured for half an hour, then have to send a thank-you note). A standard format for every interviewer is usually OK. So many notes get sent to interviewers that they probably no longer get any fun out of comparing them. The purpose of the thank-you note is: "Hey—remember me?"

What salary should you expect? According to a 1998 survey by Michigan State University, the average starting salaries of engineering grads is the highest of all majors: $44,557 for chemical engineering, $41,167 for electrical engineering, $39,857 for mechanical engineering, $39,842 for industrial engineering, and $38,741 for computer science.

Grad School

Four years of awesome problem sets, invigorating computer programming (and debugging), and lab reports has inspired you to stay in school forever and become the perpetual student (for a little fun, call yourself a "perpetual student" around your parents). Master's work typically takes approximately one to three years depending on the institution and whether it requires a thesis. Doctoral work is often a continuation of the research you did for your master's and can take up to an additional three to seven years after your master's degree (again depending on what school you go to and what you are researching).

While many students go straight from undergrad to graduate school to do a masters and possibly a Ph.D., just as many take time off before heading back to the academic setting. If you aren't certain about what area interests you or even sure what degree you want, the best thing to do is to take time off. Get a job, climb a mountain, maybe both. Too many folks find themselves in graduate school burned out and frustrated by their lowly graduate-student financial situation.

So if you decide to be grad school bound (straight or not so straight out of undergrad school), start early!

Scads of Grad School Guidance

☺ *Talk to a professor who can give you good advice (knows the area in which you are interested).* Even after reading a dozen brochures, it can be really difficult to find the schools that do good research and work in the area in which you want to specialize. Some of the least likely schools can have the best programs for what you are interested in. Professors are very

143

CHAPTER 11
*Beyond the Bachelor's
Degree—Things
to Think About
Midway Through*

well connected in their fields through societies, conferences, and meetings. They can help you find the school that will best match your interests and give you contacts.

☺ *Spend time researching schools.* The best time to look around is the summer before your senior year. Write for graduate course catalogs, a guide of the faculty's research activities, and so on. Look on the Web for more detailed outlines of professors' (and their current students') research activities. If you can, visit the schools and talk to current grad students. Besides the academic strengths and pressures, take note of quality of life and cost of living.

☺ *Apply for fellowships and grants.* Most engineering grad schools find funding for their grad students, but some do not. Look into and apply for independent funding offered by foundations (such as the Whitaker Foundation for biomechanics) or the government (such as the National Science Foundation or the Department of Defense). Independent funding makes you much more attractive to potential graduate schools and you will have fewer financial concerns. Your department administrator can usually direct you to a professor who is familiar with available fellowships. The Web is also an excellent source for scholarship, fellowship, and grant information. A good web site at which to start is FinAid, the Financial Aid Information Page, sponsored by the National Association of Student Financial Aid Administrators:

http://www.finaid.org

This will send you to its home page. Look under "graduate" for specific disciplinary searches and databases.

☺ Get research experience.

Basic research is what I'm doing when I don't know what I am doing.
—Wernher von Braun
German/American rocket engineer (1912–1977)

Most undergrads don't do research, which makes getting experience difficult (because you might have to prove yourself) and at the same time easy (because you are probably one of few undergrads interested). Research entails hunting down a professor who is doing something you think is pretty cool (check out professors' web pages to find out about their areas or research), telling them you are really interested in a specific project and asking if there is any way you can get involved. Most schools offer credit for research (a.k.a. Independent Study or Directed Study in course-cataloguese). The downside is that you may spend many more hours of research than credit hours received and will most likely have to do the bottom-of-the-tallest-totem-pole work. The good news is that you are gaining research experience that grad schools value, knowledge of a side to engineering the books can't cover, a killer addition to your resume, and a reference for your grad school application.

144

CHAPTER 11
Beyond the Bachelor's
Degree—Things
to Think About
Midway Through

☺ *Get teaching assistant (TA) experience.* If you think you may be looking for funding from your grad school, having TA experience may help you land a teaching assistantship. TAing also really helps you learn the material inside out and allows you to torture others the way you were once tortured.

☺ *Buy a GRE book.* Get out your number 2 pencil! Yes, we gifted left-brainers take the GRE (Graduate Record Examination) with all the psychology, art history, and Spanish majors who are also going to grad school. It is the SAT (Student Achievement Test) revived in graduate form except the GRE has three sections instead of two: math, verbal, and analytical. Each section is worth 800 points and the math section is rumored to be easier than the SAT. The verbal section has generally the same format as the SAT. The analytical section is logic games that simplify tremendously with a diagram or two. Go ahead and get your hands on a recommended GRE review book; even though the math and analytical parts should be fairly easy, your score reflects how you think, not how smart you are. If you did well on the SAT, you will do well on the GRE. If you wish you had done better on the SAT, you *will* do better on the GRE—just spend some time going through the review guide.

☺ *Pinpoint what you want.* Consider what this advanced degree will really give you. Do you *really* want to do more problem sets? Graduate programs are very different from school to school. Some programs can be completed in a year, do not require a thesis, and have only a specified number of classroom units in a concentration of your choice. A master's program with a thesis almost always takes longer because students are working at their own pace instead of the school's. If you think you may be interested in getting a Ph.D., be aware that students usually stay at the same school (same research project, but extended or more in-depth). So choose your school and program wisely.

☺ *Follow your instincts when you choose your school.* You will choose well!

The Part of the Application That Always Gets Left Until Last: The Essay!

Rumor has it that graduate schools use the essay primarily to check out your competence with the English language. There—that should take the pressure off. What gets you into graduate schools are your recommendations, grades, and GRE scores. The admissions committee (or individual) that reads your essay is attempting to get a sense of who you are by learning what important or beneficial engineering work you have done, what you are interested in studying further, and why you want to go to that school. A good outline to follow in your essay if you don't have any better ideas is:

1. Something that tells the school about you and how you became an engineer.
2. Why you want to go to this school (based on point 1) and what area you are interested in researching or studying further.
3. How your assets and accomplishments directly benefit the school (based on point 2). Don't be bashful. Sell yourself!
4. How attending this school fulfills all your dreams (based on 1, 2, and some literary license).

Once you get a B.E. or a B.S. in an engineering field, you are an engineer—no matter how far you try to run. Lately the most common nonengineering path for graduating engineers is the consulting world where the word "analyst" is usually somewhere in the official job title. Other not-really engineers:

- Are *sales reps* for firms that need people with technical knowledge.
- Become *technical writers.*
- Go to professional schools (*doctors, lawyers, MBAs*).
- Are often the *innovative folks* (i.e., entrepreneurs) who start up their own companies.

A surprisingly large number of engineering grads do not take "trench engineering" jobs. Engineers are a commodity to the corporate world for many reasons: first, they are problem solvers with a good tool set of analytical skills and approaches, and second, because they are used to working their @#$es off.

The hunting process for a nonengineering job differs little from the engineering job search, so . . . get internships! Utilize the career center and connections! Polish your communication skills!

Whichever path you take. . .

Good Luck!

Appendix A
Discipline-Specific
Engineering Societies

	Organization	Web site
AAEE	American Academy of Environemental Engineers	www.enviro-engrs.org
ACerS	The American Ceramic Society	www.acers.org
ACSM	American Congress on Surveying and Mapping	www.landsurveyor.com/acsm
ACEC	American Consulting Engineers	www.acec.org
ADDA	American Design Drafting Association	www.adda.org
AHS	American Helicopter Society	www.vtol.org
AIAA	American Institute of Aeronautics and Astronautics (AIAA)	www.aiaa.org
AIChE	American Institute of Chemical Engineers	www.aiche.org
ANS	American Nuclear Society	www.ans.org
ASAE	American Society of Agricultural Engineers	www.asae.org
ASCE	American Society of Civil Engineers	www.asce.org
ASEE	American Society for Engineering Education	www.asee.org
ASEM	American Society for Engineering Management	www.asem.org
ASHRAE	American Society of Heating, Refrigerating and Air-Conditioning Engineers	www.ashrae.org
ASME	The American Society of Mechanical Engineers	www.asme.org
ASNE	American Society of Naval Engineers	www.jhuapl.edu/ASNE
ASNT	The American Society for Nondestructive Testing	www.asnt.org
ASQ	American Society for Quality	www.asq.org
ASSE	American Society of Safety Engineers	www.asse.org
ASSE	American Society of Sanitary Engineering	www.asse-plumbing.org
ASTM	American Society for Testing Materials	www.astm.org
ASES	American Solar Energy Society	www.ases.org/solar
AEI	Architectural Engineering Institute	www.aeinstitute.org
ASM	ASM International	www.asm-intl.org
AACE	Association for Advancement of Cost Engineering	www.aacei.org
ACM	Association for Computing Machinery	www.acm.org
AEE	Association of Energy Engineers	www.aeecenter.org
AISE	Association of Iron and Steel Engineers	www.aise.org
AES	Audio Engineering Society	www.aes.org
BMES	Biomedical Engineering Society	www.mecca.org/BME/BMES/ society/bmeshm.html
CSA	Cryogenic Society of America	www-csa.fnal.gov
IESNA	Illuminating Engineering Society of North America	www.iesna.org
IEEE	The Institute of Electronics and Electrical Engineers	www.ieee.org
IIE	Institute of Industrial Engineers	www.iienet.org
INFORMS	Institute for Operations Research and the Management Sciences	www.informs.org
IMAPS	International Microelectronics and Packaging Society	www.imaps@imaps.org
ISA	International Society for Measurement and Control	www.isa.org
SPIE	The International Society for Optical Engineering	www.spie.org
MRS	The Materials Research Society	www.mrs.org
TMS	The Minerals Metals and Materials Society	www.tms.org
NAWIC	National Association of Women in Construction	www.nawic.org
OSA	Optical Society of America	www.osa.org
SAE	The Society of Automotive Engineers	www.sae.org
SEM	Society for Experimental Mechanics	www.sem.org
SFPE	Society of Fire Protection Engineers	www.sfpe.org
SIAM	Society for Industrial and Applied Mathematics	www.siam.org
SME	Society of Manufacturing Engineers	www.sme.org
SNAME	Society of Naval Architects & Marine Engineers	www.sname.org
SPE	Society of Petroleum Engineers	www.spe.org
SPE	Society of Plastics Engineers	www.4spe.org
SES	Standards Engineering Society	www.ses-standards.org/
WEF	Water Environment Federation	www.wef.org

Key: N = not available, n/a = not applicable, G = student members are part of general membership.

E-mail	Telephone	Total Members	Student Chapters
aaee@ea.net	(410) 266-3311	2,300+	N
info@acers.org	(614) 794-5890	10,000+	37
infoacsm@mindspring.com	(310) 493-0200	N	N
acec@acec.org	(202) 347-7474	5,700	0
national@adda.org	(301) 460-6875	2,000	57
AHS703@aol.com	(703) 684-6777	6,000	10
custserv@aiaa.org	(800) 639-2422	30,000	140+
xpress@aiche.org	(800) AICHEME	54,500	148
outreach@ans.org	(708) 352-6611	13,000	51
hq@asae.org	(616) 429-0300	9,000	83
N	(800) 548-2723	120,000+	224
membership@asee.org	(202) 331-3520	10,000	6
asemmsd@rollanet.org	(573) 341-2101	1,300	5
orders@ashrae.org	(800) 527-4723	50,000	145
infocentral@asme.org	(800) THE-ASME	125,000	1,000
jowen.asne@mcimail.com	(703) 836-6727	6,000	5
N	(614) 274-6003	10,000	n/a
cs@asq.org	(800) 248-1946	136,000+	66
customerservice@asse.org	(847) 699-2929	32,000	54
ASSE@IX.netcom.com	(440) 835-3040	2,800	G
service@astm.org	(610) 832-9585	35,000	n/a
ases@ases.org	(303) 443-3130	6,000	3
cbelcher@ukans.edu	(703) 295-6017	3,000	12
Mem-Serv@po.ASM-Intl.org	(800) 336-5152	43,000	100+
74757.2636@compuserve.com	(304) 296-8444	5,500	6
acmhelp@acm.org	(800) 342-6626	80,000+	430
info@AEEcenter.org	(770) 447-5083	8,000+	G
membership@aise.org	(412) 281-6323	11,000	n/a
HQ@aes.org	(212) 661-8528	N	N
bmes@netcom.com	(310) 618-9322	N	N
csa@huget.com	(708) 383-6220	500	G
iesna@iesna.org	(212) 248-5000 ext. 101	8,000	23
member.services@ieee.org	(800) 678-4333	320,000	950
cs@www.iienet.org	(770) 449-0461	24,000	161
informs@informs.org	(800)446-3676	11,000	48
imaps@imaps.org	(888) GO-IMAPS	7,000	26
info@isa.org	(919) 549-8411	50,000+	n/a
spie@spie.org	(360) 676-3290	13,000+	13
info@mrs.org	(724) 779-3003	12,400	39
tmsgeneral@tms.org	(724) 776-9000	13,000	90
nawic@onramp.net	(800) 552-3506	6,500	G
osamem@osa.org	(202) 223-8130	n/a	26
davids@sae.org	(412) 776-4841	75,000	310
sem@sem1.com	(203) 790-6373	3,000	8
sfpehqtrs@sfpe.org	(301) 718-2910	4,600	4
siam@siam.org	(215) 382-9800	9,000	G
wertzri@sme.org	(800) 733-4763	70,000	240
eromanelli@sname.org	(800) 798-2188	10,000+	13
chadowski@spelink.spe.org	(972) 952-9316	12,000	82
4spemail@4spe.org	(203) 775-0471	35,000	100
hgziggy@worldnet.att.net	(305) 971-4798	N	N
msc@wef.org	(800) 888-0206	40,000+	G

Appendix B
Special Interest Societies

Organization	
Ethnic societies	
AABEA	American Association of Bangladeshi Engineers & Architects
AISES	American Indian Science and Engineering Society
BDPA	Black Data Processors Associates
CAHSEE	Center for the Advancement of Hispanics in Science and Engineering Education
CESASC	Chinese-American Engineers and Scientists Association of Southern California
HAES	Haitian-American Engineering Society
NACME	National Action Council for Minorities in Engineering
NSBE	National Society of Black Engineers
SACNAS	Society for the Advancement of Chicanos and Native Americans in Science
SHPE	Society of Hispanic Professional Engineers
MAES	Society of Mexican American Engineers and Scientists
VACETS	Vietnamese Association for Computing, Engineering Technology and Science
Special interest societies and organizations	
AWC	Association for Women in Computing
E Week	National Engineers Week web site
JETS	Junior Engineering Technical Society
NAWIC	National Association of Women in Construction
NCEES	National Council of Examiners for Engineering and Surveying
NSPE	National Society of Professional Engineers
SWE	Society of Women Engineers

Key: N = not available.

Web site	E-mail	Phone
cse.eng.lmu.edu/~aabea/	nula@cse.eng.lmu.edu	N
bioc02.uthsca.edu/aisesnet.html	AISESHQ@spot.colorado.edu	(303) 939-0023
www.bdpa.org	nbdpa@ix.netcom.net	(202) 789-1540
www.seas.gwu.edu/student/ cahsee/homepage.html	cahsee@seas.gwu.edu	(301) 299-0033
www.cesasc.org	webmaster@cesasc.org	N
www.haiti-science.com/haes/	haes@haiti-science.com	(305) 621-1189
www.nacme.org	information@www.nacme.org	(212) 279-2626
www.nsbe.org	member@nsbehq.nsbe.org	(703) 549-2207 ext.210
www.sacnas.org	sacnas@cats.ucsc.edu	(408) 459-4272
www.shpe.org	shpenational@shpe.org	(213) 725-3970
www.tamu.edu/maes	maes@tamu.edu	(310) 618-1344
www.vacets.org	vacets-adcom@vacets.org	(703) 760-9198
www.awc-hq.org	awc@awc-hq.org	(415) 905-4663
www.eweek.org	eweek@nspe.org	(703) 684-2852
www.asee.org/jets	jets@nas.edu	(703) 548-5387
www.nawic.org	nawic@onramp.net	(800) 552-3506
www.ncees.org	N	(800) 250-3196
www.nspe.org	customer.service@nspe.org	(888) 285-NSPE
www.swe.org	vp-student.services@swe.org	(212) 509-9577

Appendix C
Engineering Honor Societies

Organization	Discipline
Alpha Epsilon	Agricultural Engineering
Alpha Eta Mu Beta	Biomedical
Alpha Eta Rho	Aviation
Alpha Mu	Agricultural Mechanization
Alpha Nu Sigma	Nuclear Engineering
Alpha Pi Mu	Industrial
Alpha Sigma Mu	Material Sciences
Beta Beta Beta	Biological Sciences
Beta Tau Epsilon	Manufacturing
Chi Epsilon	Civil
Delta Nu Alpha	Transportation
Epsilon Delta Sigma	Management Engineering
Epsilon Lambda Chi	Engineering Leadership
Epsilon Pi Eta	Environmental Health Studies
Epsilon Pi Tau	Research in Technology
Eta Kappa Nu	Electrical Engineering
Kappa Theta Epsilon	Co-op
Keramos	Ceramics
Gamma Epsilon	General Engineering
Gamma Sigma Delta	Agriculture
Lambda Tau	Medical Technology
Omega Chi Epsilon	Chemical Engineering
Omega Rho	Operations Research
Omicron Kappa Pi	Architecture
Order of St. Patrick	Engineering Leadership
Phi Lambda Upsilon	Chemical Engineering
Phi Psi	Textiles
Pi Alpha Epsilon	Building Construction
Pi Alpha Xi	Horticulture
Pi Epsilon Tau	Petroleum Engineering
Pi Mu Epsilon	Mathematics
Pi Tau Sigma	Mechanical Engineering
Sigma Gamma Epsilon	Geological and Mining Engineering
Sigma Gamma Tau	Aerospace and Aeronautical Engineering
Sigma Lambda Chi	Building Construction
Sigma Pi Epsilon	Plastics Engineering
Sigma Pi Sigma	Physics
Sigma Xi	Engineering and Scientific Research
Tau Beta Pi	National Engineering Society
Tau Sigma Delta	Architecture and Allied Arts
Upsilon Phi Epsilon	Computer Science
Xi Sigma Pi	Forestry

For more information on engineering honor societies see your advisor.

Appendix D
Some Useful Stuff

Logarithms

$$\log_b xy = \log_b x + \log_b y$$

$$\log_b \left(\frac{x}{y}\right) = \log_b x = \log_b y$$

$$\log_b x^y = y \log_b x$$

Formulas for Common Shapes

Circle

$$C = 2 \pi r$$

$$A = \pi r^2$$

Ellipse

$$C = 2 \pi \sqrt{\frac{a^2 + b^2}{2}}$$

$$A = \pi a b$$

Cylinder

$$A = 2 \pi r (h + r)$$

$$V = \pi r^2 h$$

Sphere

$$A = 4 \pi r^2$$

$$V = \frac{4}{3} \pi r^3$$

Greek Alphabet

Alpha	A	α	Nu	N	ν
Beta	B	β	Xi	Ξ	ξ
Gamma	Γ	γ	Omicron	O	o
Delta	Δ	δ	Pi	Π	π
Epsilon	E	ϵ	Rho	P	ρ
Zeta	Z	ζ	Sigma	Σ	σ
Eta	H	η	Tau	T	τ
Theta	Θ	θ	Upsilon	Y	υ
Iota	I	ι	Phi	Φ	ϕ
Kappa	K	κ	Chi	X	χ
Lambda	Λ	λ	Psi	Ψ	ψ
Mu	M	μ	Omega	Ω	ω

Dimensional Prefixes

Symbol	Prefix	Multiple
T	tera units	10^{12}
G	giga units	10^{9}
M	mega units	10^{6}
k	kilo units	10^{3}
h	hecto units	10^{2}
da	deca units	10^{1}
	(no prefix) units	10^{0}
d	deci units	10^{-1}
c	centi units	10^{-2}
m	milli units	10^{-3}
μ	micro units	10^{-6}
n	nano units	10^{-9}
p	pico units	10^{-12}
f	femto units	10^{-15}
a	atto units	10^{-18}

Periodic Table of the Elements

Legend:
- Atomic number → Element
- Symbol
- Atomic weight based on $C^{12} = 12.00$
- ( ) denotes mass number of most stable known isotope

Categories shown: Light metals · Brittle metals · Ductile metals · Low melting · Nonmetallic elements · Inert gases · Rare earth elements · Lanthanide series · Actinide series · Transuranium elements

1	2	3	4	5	6	7	8	9	10	11	12	13	14	15	16	17	18
1 Hydrogen H 1.00797																	2 Helium He 4.003
3 Lithium Li 6.941	4 Beryllium Be 9.0122											5 Boron B 10.811	6 Carbon C 12.01	7 Nitrogen N 14.00	8 Oxygen O 15.999	9 Fluorine F 18.998	10 Neon Ne 20.18
11 Sodium Na 22.9898	12 Magnesium Mg 24.305											13 Aluminum Al 26.98	14 Silicon Si 28.086	15 Phosphorus P 30.97	16 Sulfur S 32.06	17 Chlorine Cl 35.453	18 Argon Ar 39.948
19 Potassium K 39.098	20 Calcium Ca 40.08	21 Scandium Sc 44.956	22 Titanium Ti 47.87	23 Vanadium V 50.942	24 Chromium Cr 51.996	25 Manganese Mn 54.938	26 Iron Fe 55.847	27 Cobalt Co 58.9332	28 Nickel Ni 58.69	29 Copper Cu 63.546	30 Zinc Zn 65.39	31 Gallium Ga 69.72	32 Germanium Ge 72.59	33 Arsenic As 74.92	34 Selenium Se 78.96	35 Bromine Br 79.904	36 Krypton Kr 83.80
37 Rubidium Rd 85.47	38 Strontium Sr 87.62	39 Yttrium Y 88.906	40 Zirconium Zr 91.22	41 Niobium Nb 92.906	42 Molybdenum Mo 95.94	43 Technetium Tc (98)	44 Ruthenium Ru 101.07	45 Rhodium Rh 103.905	46 Palladium Pd 106.4	47 Silver Ag 107.868	48 Cadmium Cd 112.41	49 Indium In 114.82	50 Tin Sn 118.71	51 Antimony Sb 121.76	52 Tellurium Te 127.60	53 Iodine I 126.90	54 Xenon Xe 131.29
55 Cesium Cs 132.905	56 Barium Ba 137.34	57 Lanthanum La 137.91	72 Hafnium Hf 178.49	73 Tantalum Ta 180.948	74 Tungsten W 183.84	75 Rhenium Re 186.2	76 Osmium Os 190.2	77 Iridium Ir 192.2	78 Platinum Pt 195.08	79 Gold Au 196.97	80 Mercury Hg 200.59	81 Thallium Tl 204.38	82 Lead Pb 207.19	83 Bismuth Bi 208.98	84 Polonium Po (209)	85 Astatine At (210)	86 Radon Rn (222)
87 Francium Fr (223)	88 Radium Ra (226)	89 Actinium Ac (227)															

LANTHANIDE SERIES

58 Cerium Ce 140.12	59 Praseodymium Pr 140.907	60 Neodymium Nd 144.24	61 Promethium Pm (145)	62 Samarium Sm 150.36	63 Europium Eu 151.96	64 Gadolinium Gd 157.25	65 Terbium Tb 158.924	66 Dysprosium Dy 162.50	67 Holmium Ho 164.93	68 Erbium Er 167.26	69 Thulium Tm 168.934	70 Ytterbium Yb 173.04	71 Lutetium Lu 174.97

ACTINIDE SERIES

90 Thorium Th 232.038	91 Protactinium Pa 231.04	92 Uranium U 238.03	93 Neptunium Np (237)	94 Plutonium Pu (244)	95 Americium Am (243)	96 Curium Cm (247)	97 Berkelium Bk (247)	98 Californium Cf (251)	99 Einsteinium Es (252)	100 Fermium Fm (257)	101 Mendelevium Md (258)	102 Nobelium No (259)	103 Lawrencium Lr (262)

Note: For more information on the elements, log onto "Periodic Table of Elements on the Internet" at: domains.twave.net/domain/yinon/default.html.

Trigonometry—Right Angled Triangle

1. $\dfrac{\text{Opposite Side}}{\text{Hypotenuse}} = \text{Sine } \theta \qquad \dfrac{O}{H} = \sin \theta$

2. $\dfrac{\text{Adjacent Side}}{\text{Hypotenuse}} = \text{Cosine } \theta \qquad \dfrac{A}{H} = \cos \theta$

3. $\dfrac{\text{Opposite Side}}{\text{Adjacent Side}} = \text{Tangent } \theta \qquad \dfrac{O}{A} = \tan \theta$

4. $\dfrac{\text{Adjacent Side}}{\text{Opposite Side}} = \text{Cotangent } \theta \qquad \dfrac{A}{O} = \cot \theta$

5. $\dfrac{\text{Hypotenuse}}{\text{Adjacent Side}} = \text{Secant } \theta \qquad \dfrac{H}{A} = \sec \theta$

6. $\dfrac{\text{Hypotenuse}}{\text{Opposite Side}} = \text{Cosecant } \theta \qquad \dfrac{H}{O} = \csc \theta$

Fundamental relations

7. $\sin \theta = \theta - \dfrac{\theta^3}{3!} + \dfrac{\theta^5}{5!} - \dfrac{\theta^7}{7!} - \dfrac{\theta^9}{9!} \cdots$

8. $\cos \theta = 1 - \dfrac{\theta^2}{2!} + \dfrac{\theta^4}{4!} - \dfrac{\theta^6}{6!} + \dfrac{\theta^8}{8!} \cdots$

9. $\sin^2 \theta = \cos^2 \theta + 1$

10. $\sin^2 \theta = \dfrac{1}{2} - \dfrac{1}{2} \cos 2\theta$

11. $\cos^2 \theta = \dfrac{1}{2} + \dfrac{1}{2} \cos 2\theta$

12. $\sec^2 \theta - \tan^2 \theta = 1$

13. $\csc^2 \theta - \cot^2 \theta = 1$

14. $\sin n\theta = 2 \sin (n - 1)\theta \cos \theta - \sin (n - 2)\theta$

15. $\cos n\theta = 2 \cos (n - 1)\theta \cos \theta - \cos (n - 2)\theta$

16. $\sin 2\theta = 2 \sin \theta \cos \theta$

17. $\cos 2\theta = 2 \cos^2 \theta - 1 = 1 - 2 \sin^2 \theta = \cos^2 \theta - \sin^2 \theta$

18. $\sin (\theta \pm \alpha) = \sin \theta \cos \alpha \pm \cos \theta \sin \alpha$

19. $\cos (\theta \pm \alpha) = \cos \theta \cos \alpha \mp \sin \theta \sin \alpha$

20. $\tan (\theta \pm \alpha) = \dfrac{\tan \theta \pm \tan \alpha}{1 \mp \tan \theta \tan \alpha}$

21. $\sin \theta = \sqrt{1 - \cos^2 \theta} = \dfrac{\tan \theta}{\sqrt{1 + \tan^2 \theta}} = \cos \theta \tan \theta = \sqrt{\dfrac{1}{2}(1 - \cos 2\theta)}$

22. $\cos \theta = \sqrt{1 - \sin^2 \theta} = \dfrac{1}{\sqrt{1 + \tan^2 \theta}} = \sin \theta \cot \theta = \sqrt{\dfrac{1}{2}(1 + \cos 2\theta)}$

23. $\tan \theta = \dfrac{\sin \theta}{\sqrt{1 - \sin^2 \theta}} = \dfrac{\sqrt{1 - \cos^2 \theta}}{\cos \theta} = \dfrac{\sin 2\theta}{1 + \cos 2\theta} = \dfrac{2 \tan \theta/2}{1 - \tan^2 \theta/2}$

24. $\sin \theta/2 = \sqrt{\dfrac{1 - \cos \theta}{2}}$

25. $\cos \theta/2 = \sqrt{\dfrac{1 + \cos \theta}{2}}$

26. $\tan \theta/2 = \dfrac{1 - \cos \theta}{\sin \theta} = \sqrt{\dfrac{1 - \cos \theta}{1 + \cos \theta}}$

Specific Gravities and Specific Weights

Material	Average Specific Gravity	Average Specific Weight lb_f/ft^3	Material	Average Specific Gravity	Average Specific Weight lb_f/ft^3
Acid, sulfuric, 87%	1.80	112	Iron, gray cast	7.10	450
Air, S.T.P.	0.001293	0.0806	Iron, wrought	7.75	480
Alcohol, ethyl	0.790	49	Kerosene	0.80	50
Aluminum, cast	2.65	165			
Asbestos	2.5	153	Lead	11.34	710
Ash, white	0.67	42	Leather	0.94	59
Ashes, cinders	0.68	44	Limestone, solid	2.70	168
Asphaltum	1.3	81	Limestone, crushed	1.50	95
Babbitt metal, soft	10.25	625	Mahogany	0.70	44
Basalt, granite	1.50	96	Manganese	7.42	475
Brass, cast-rolled	8.50	534	Marble	2.70	166
Brick, common	1.90	119	Mercury	13.56	845
Bronze, 7.9 to 14% S_n	8.1	509	Monel metal, rolled	8.97	555
Cedar, white, red	0.35	22	Nickel	8.90	558
Cement, portland, bags	1.44	90	Oak, white	0.77	48
Chalk	2.25	140	Oil, lubricating	0.91	57
Clay, dry	1.00	63			
Clay, loose, wet	1.75	110	Paper	0.92	58
Coal, anthracite, solid	1.60	95	Paraffin	0.90	56
Coal, bituminous, solid	1.35	85	Petroleum, crude	0.88	55
Concrete, gravel, sand	2.3	142	Pine, white	0.43	27
Copper, cast, rolled	8.90	556	Platinum	21.5	1330
Cork	0.24	15	Redwood, California	0.42	26
Cotton, flax, hemp	1.48	93	Rubber	1.25	78
Copper ore	4.2	262			
Earth	1.75	105	Sand, loose, wet	1.90	120
			Sandstone, solid	2.30	144
Fir, Douglas	0.50	32	Seawater	1.03	64
Flour, loose	0.45	28	Silver	10.5	655
Gasoline	0.70	44	Steel, structural	7.90	490
Glass, crown	2.60	161	Sulfur	2.00	125
Glass, flint	3.30	205	Teak, African	0.99	62
Glycerine	1.25	78	Tin	7.30	456
Gold, cast-hammered	19.3	1205	Tungsten	19.22	1200
Granite, solid	2.70	172	Turpentine	0.865	54
Graphite	1.67	135	Water, 4° C	1.00	62.4
Gravel, loose, wet	1.68	105	Water, snow, fresh fallen	0.125	8.0
Hickory	0.77	48	Zinc	7.14	445
Ice	0.91	57			

Note: The value for the specific weight of water that is usually used in problem solutions is 62.4 lb_f/ft^3 or 8.34 lb_f/gal.

Electronics Symbols

Resistor—General

Tapped

Variable

Capacitor—General

Variable

Feed-through

Antenna—General

Dipole   Loop   Counter poise

Battery

One cell   Multicell

Permanent magnet

Pickup
or head   Writing   Reading   Erasing

Piezoelectric
crystal unit

Thermocouple
(temperature measuring)

Conductive path or conductor

Air or space path

Crossing—not connected

Junction of paths
or conductors

Shielded single conductor

2 conductor cable

Coaxial cable

Ground
Earth   Chassis

Basic contact assemblies

Close contact
(break)

Open contact
(make)

Switch

Single throw   Double throw

Pushbutton

Circuit
closing

Circuit
opening

Selector or multi-
position switch

Connector
Jack—female contact

Plug—male contact

Communication connector

2 conductor jack

2 conductor plug

Power supply connector

Female

Male

Inductor—general

Magnetic core

Tapped

Adjustable

Transformer

General   Magnetic
core

Electron tube components
Directly heated
(filamentary) cathode

Indirectly heated
cathode

Cold cathode

Photo cathode

Grid

Deflecting electrodes

Anode or plate

Applications

Triode   Pentode

Gas filled
voltage regulator   Phototube

Cathode
ray tube

Semiconductor
diode

Undirectional diode

PNP Transistor

NPN Transistor

Photovoltaic transducer

Fuse

Lightning arrester

Circuit breaker

Bell

Buzzer

Loudspeaker

Microphone

Handset

Earphone

Headset

Fluorescent lamp
(4 terminal)

Glow lamp (AC type)

Incandescent lamp

Signal or indicator
light

Ammeter   Ⓐ

Voltmeter   Ⓥ

Wattmeter   Ⓦ

Generator   Ⓖ   GEN

Motor   Ⓜ   MOT

Winding connections
(motors & generators)

1 Phase

2 Phase

3 Phase wye

4 Phase delta

Guide to Fabric Care Symbols

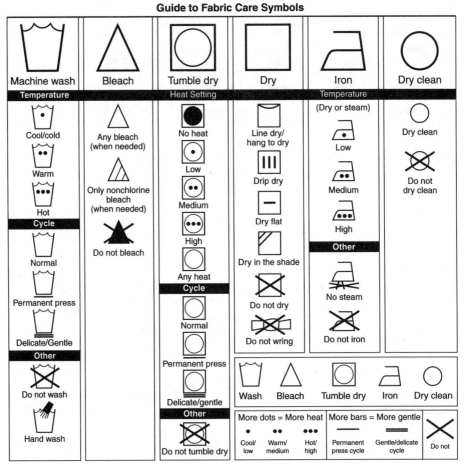

Machine wash	Bleach	Tumble dry	Dry	Iron	Dry clean

Machine wash — Temperature: Cool/cold, Warm, Hot

Machine wash — Cycle: Normal, Permanent press, Delicate/Gentle

Machine wash — Other: Do not wash, Hand wash

Bleach: Any bleach (when needed), Only nonchlorine bleach (when needed), Do not bleach

Tumble dry — Heat Setting: No heat, Low, Medium, High, Any heat

Tumble dry — Cycle: Normal, Permanent press, Delicate/gentle

Tumble dry — Other: Do not tumble dry

Dry: Line dry/hang to dry, Drip dry, Dry flat, Dry in the shade, Do not dry, Do not wring

Iron — Temperature (Dry or steam): Low, Medium, High

Iron — Other: No steam, Do not iron

Dry clean: Dry clean, Do not dry clean

Wash	Bleach	Tumble dry	Iron	Dry clean

More dots = More heat			More bars = More gentle		
• Cool/low	•• Warm/medium	••• Hot/high	— Permanent press cycle	═ Gentle/delicate cycle	✕ Do not

Courtesy of The Soap and Detergent Association.

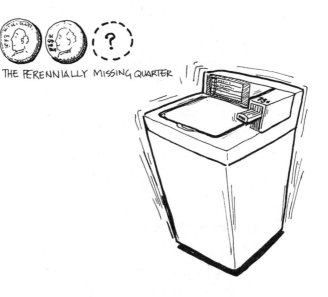

THE PERENNIALLY MISSING QUARTER

Calculus

Differential calculus formulas

1. $\dfrac{d}{dx}(x) = 1$

2. $\dfrac{d}{dx}(a) = 0$

3. $\dfrac{d}{dx}(u \pm v \mp w \pm \cdots$

$= \dfrac{du}{dx} \pm \dfrac{dv}{dx} \mp \dfrac{dw}{dx} \cdots$

4. $\dfrac{d}{dx}(au) = a\dfrac{du}{dx}$

5. $\dfrac{d}{dx}(uv) = u\dfrac{dv}{dx} + v\dfrac{du}{dx}$

6. $\dfrac{d}{dx}\left(\dfrac{u}{v}\right) = \dfrac{v\dfrac{du}{dx} - u\dfrac{dv}{dx}}{v^2}$

7. $\dfrac{d(u^n)}{dx} = nu^{n-1}\dfrac{du}{dx}$

8. $\dfrac{dy}{dx} = \dfrac{\dfrac{1}{dx}}{\dfrac{dv}{dy}} = \dfrac{\dfrac{dy}{dv}}{\dfrac{dv}{dx}}$

9. $\dfrac{d}{dx}\log_a u = \dfrac{\log_a \epsilon}{u}\dfrac{du}{dx}$

10. $\dfrac{d}{dx}\ln u = \dfrac{1}{u}\dfrac{dv}{dx}$

11. $\dfrac{d}{dx}a^u = a^u \ln a \dfrac{du}{dx}$

12. $\dfrac{d}{dx}e^u = e^u \dfrac{du}{dx}$

13. $\dfrac{d}{dx}u^v = vu^{v-1}\dfrac{du}{dx} + u^v \ln u \dfrac{dv}{dx}$

14. $\dfrac{d}{dx}\sin u = \cos u \dfrac{du}{dx}$

15. $\dfrac{d}{dx}\cos u = -\sin u \dfrac{du}{dx}$

16. $\dfrac{d}{dx}\tan u = \sec^2 u \dfrac{du}{dx}$

17. $\dfrac{d}{dx}\cot u = -\csc^2 u \dfrac{du}{dx}$

18. $\dfrac{d}{dx}\sec u = \sec u \tan u \dfrac{du}{dx}$

19. $\dfrac{d}{dx}\csc u = -\csc u \cot u \dfrac{du}{dx}$

20. $\dfrac{d}{dx}\sin^{-1} u = \dfrac{1}{\sqrt{1 - u^2}}\dfrac{du}{dx}$

21. $\dfrac{d}{dx}\cos^{-1} u = \dfrac{1}{\sqrt{1 - u^2}}\dfrac{du}{dx}$

22. $\dfrac{d}{dx}\tan^{-1} u = \dfrac{1}{1 + u^2}\dfrac{du}{dx}$

23. $\dfrac{d}{dx}\cot^{-1} u = -\dfrac{1}{1 + u^2}\dfrac{du}{dx}$

24. $\dfrac{d}{dx}\sec^{-1} u = \dfrac{1}{\sqrt[u]{u^2 - 1}}\dfrac{du}{dx}$

25. $\dfrac{d}{dx}\csc^{-1} u = -\dfrac{1}{\sqrt[u]{u^2 - 1}}\dfrac{du}{dx}$

Note: u and v = functions of x
a, e, and n = constants.

Appendix E
Sample Resume

Penny Gadget

Box 7065, Graceland, TN 94309   (555) 497-9699
gadget@widget.acme.edu
www.acme.edu\students\pgadget

EDUCATION

8/96–present	**Acme University,** Graceland, TN
	B.E. in Environmental Engineering, 3.2/4.0, Expected graduation 6/00
8/92–5/96	**Seacrest High School,** Sanibel, CA
	Graduated Third in class, 3.6/4.0 GPA

HONORS

1996	**Seacrest High School Student-Athlete of the Year**

ACTIVITIES

1996–present	**American Society of Civil Engineers,** *Vice President* (1997–98)
1996–present	**Student Newspaper "American Acme,"** *Science Editor*, weekly column "Ask the Science Bug"
1996–present	**Helping Hands,** Student-run community service group that assists in local homeless shelters.
1992–1996	**Seacrest Biology Club,** President (1995–96), Sanibel, CA
1992–1996	**Seacrest Varsity Tennis Team,** Captain (1995–96), Sanibel, CA

EXPERIENCE

6/97–9/97	*Environmental Engineering Intern,* **Eastbay Water Management,** Eastbay, CA
	Assisted professional engineers with review of surface water permits. Performed site checks and investigated permit infractions.
8/96–3/97	*Head Tennis Instructor,* **Drummond Family Tennis Centre,** Sanibel, CA
	Taught lessons daily to adults and children. Organized and ran two statewide tournaments.
9/96–12/96	*Research Assistant,* **Acme University Department of Earth Sciences,** Graceland, TN
	Assisted graduate students with data collection and analysis. Cataloged journal articles.

COMPUTER SKILLS

Mathematica, C, Matlab, HTML, and Autocad
PC and Macintosh literate.

REFERENCES

Available on request

Bibliography—
Thanks for the Info!

Chapter 2
National Society for Professional Engineers (NSPE) Web site.

Chapter 4
Gough, Paddy W. "The Female Engineering Student: What Makes Her Tick?" In *Proceedings of the Conference on Women in Engineering June 22 to 25, 1975.* Ithaca, N.Y.: Cornell University, 1975.

Holmstrom, Engin Inel. "The New Pioneers . . . Women Engineering Students." In *Proceedings of the Conference on Women in Engineering, June 22 to 25, 1975.* Ithaca, N.Y.: Cornell University, 1975.

Matyas, Marsha Lakes, and Shirley M. Malcom, eds. *Investing in Human Potential: Science and Engineering at the Crossroads.* Washington, D.C.: American Association for the Advancement of Science, 1991.

National Research Council. *Engineering Education: Designing an Adaptive System.* Washington, D.C.: National Academy Press, 1995.

O'Brannon, Helen. "The Social Scene: Isolation and Frustration." In *Proceedings of the Conference on Women in Engineering, June 22 to 25, 1975.* Ithaca, N.Y.: Cornell University, 1975.

Ott, Mary Diederich. "Attitudes and Experiences of Freshman Engineers at Cornell." In *Proceedings of the Conference on Women in Engineering, June 22 to 25, 1975.* Ithaca, N.Y.: Cornell University, 1975.

Ott, Mary Diederich, and Nancy A. Reese, eds. *Women in Engineering . . . Beyond Recruitment.* Proceedings of the Conference, Cornell University, Ithaca, June 22 to 25, 1975.

Reamon, Derek. Research presentation, Stanford University, 1998.

Shields, Charles J. *Back in School: A Guide for Adult Learners.* Hawthorne, N.J.: Career Press, 1994.

Siebert, Al, and Bernadine Gilpin. *The Adult Student's Guide to Survival and Success,* 3rd ed. Portland, Oreg.: Practical Psychology Press, 1996.

Chapter 5
Vanderbilt University. Vanderbilt University Undergraduate Catalog Bulletin, 1994–95.

Chapter 6

Vanderbilt University. Fall 1992 "CE 180 syllabus" (modeled after).

Chapter 7

Brown, John Fiske. *A Student Guide to Engineering Report Writing.* Solana Beach, Calif.: United Western Press, 1985.

Faste, Rolfe. Class notes from ME 116B. (Mind map information). Stanford University, Winter 1997.

Harvill, Lawrence R., and Thomas L. Kraft. *Technical Report Standards: How to Prepare and Write Effective Technical Reports.* Forest Grove, Oreg.: M/A Press, 1978.

Holman, J. P., and W. J. Gajda, Jr. *Experimental Methods for Engineers*, 5th ed. New York: McGraw-Hill, 1989.

Robinson, Adam. *What Smart Students Know: Maximum Grades, Optimum Learning, Minimum Time.* NewYork: Crown Publishers, 1993.

Chapter 8

Robinson, Adam. *What Smart Students Know: Maximum Grades, Optimum Learning, Minimum Time.* New York: Crown Publishers, 1993.

Chapter 9

Columbia University. Go Ask Alice, Web site, Student Health Center, Columbia University,

Duke University. Healthy Devil Web site, Student Health Center, Duke University,

Huffman, Karen; Mark Vernoy; Barbara Williams; and Judith Vernoy. *Psychology in Action*, 2nd ed. New York: John Wiley & Sons, 1991.

Chapter 10

Franklin, Benjamin. *The Autobiography of Benjamin Franklin.* Cambridge, Mass.: Houghton Mifflin, 1928.

Root-Berstein, Robert Scott. "Visual Thinking: The Art of Imagining Reality." *Transactions of the American Philosophical Society* 75 (Part 6), 1985.

McTutor's History of Mathematics Web site, http:/www-groups.dcs.st-and.ac.uk/ ~history/.

Chapter 11

National Society of Professional Engineers (NSPE) Web site, http://www.nspe.org/ lc-home.htm.

Stanford Career Planning and Placement Center. Resume handouts.

Stanford University. "Career Steps" Handout, Ambidextrous Thinking ME 313 (Engineering interviews), Fall 1995.

Appendix C

Holman, J. P., and W. J. Gajda, Jr. *Experimental Methods for Engineers,* 5th ed. New York: McGraw-Hill, 1989.

To Mom and Dad (of course)

Acknowledgments

The author wishes to thank the following people for their input, time, ideas, and patience: Marlene and John Donaldson for knowing this book as well as I do; Oliver Fringer for his thoughtfulness in review, and his patience, excitement, and unwavering encouragement; Janay Johnson for being everything a most dear friend is; Michal Pasternak for her time, thoughtfulness, and wonderful sense of humor; Elizabeth Loboa for sharing her experiences, her assistance at every stage of writing, and her enthusiastic and unending support; the Stanford Product Design Loft for patience, paper, and punchiness; Juliana Aldous for her many encouraging and insightful answers to my many questions; Dan Kim for being fun and talented; Carla Cloutier for being a very cool engineer and my only sibling; Professor Bernie Roth and my ME215 cohorts of Stanford University (you know who you are . . .) for encouragement, providing me a means to work on this text as "schoolwork," and changing the way I view the world; D'Andre Davis, Leshell Hatley, Rama Polefka, and Shannon Dunn for providing insight and relating their experiences; Evan S. Bowen for noisy Saturday afternoon CS chats in the model shop; Maryanne Weiss of ABET for answering my questions and her continued interest; Professor Jim Adams, Stanford University, for having a big grin whenever I see him and for getting the ball rolling; Karen Brothers and Amanda Lenay for their thoughtful input; Meg Wiley for consideration in her review and for her love of engineering pedagogy; Professor David Freyberg, Stanford University, for being interested in and excited about my project, Bryan Cooperrider and Craig Milroy for their wit and feedback; Kate Milroy for her time and for catching 3E8 when many engineers missed it; Matt Brennan for sending tidbits he thought were relevant (they always were); Professors Rolf Faste, Sara Little Turnbull, David Kelley, and Matt Kahn of Stanford University because Product Design relates strongly to book writing; Professors Thomas Cruse, Alvin Strauss, John Williamson, and Carol Rubin of Vanderbilt University whose teachings are most likely reflected in this book as they taught me engineering; the Fort Myers Center of South

Florida Water Management, especially Jacque Grahmn, for giving me my first exposure to engineering; Bill Kauffman and Pip & Poop for their excellent input and advice on entering the world of publishers; Bill and Marty Lucas for their constant support and wisdom; Professors Sheri Sheppard and Dave Beach of Stanford University for being excellent role models and for making being a student unquestionably fun; my Nairobi flatmates Olga Bornemisza and Ele Pawelski for advice and use of their e-mail accounts; and Dr. Martin Fisher and Mawk Butcher of ApproTEC for their knowledgeable (and creative) input; Cappy MacDonald for her attentive review; Art and Dee Kauffman for kind support; Dan D. Budny of Purdue University, Bruce R. Dewey of University of Wyoming, James H. Garrett of Carnegie Mellon University, Byron Gottfried of University of Pittsburgh, Rick Olson of University of San Diego, and Thomas Walker of VPI for sound advice and excellent reviews; and last, but certainly not least, the folks at McGraw-Hill: Holly Stark, Kim Schau, Eric Munson, Leah Thompson, and George Haag, all of whom patiently answered my many questions, allowed me to be stubborn, were flexible with my hectic quarter and changing ideas, and were great to work with. THANKS!

Dan Kim would like to thank his loving parents and big brother; his oldest, best friend for life, Woo-young Rhee; and George Kembel and Pete Richards for crazy ideas and scary formulas.

About the Author

KRISTA DONALDSON graduated from Vanderbilt University in 1995 with a bachelors in Mechanical Engineering. She went on to Stanford University where she discovered the machine shop and the main reason she had wanted to become an engineer—to make stuff! This took her into the Stanford Product Design (joint masters program in Art and Mechanical Engineering) where she was able to design and produce cool things—like an ice cream cone mold and a chandelier that doubles as a swing. Having graduated recently with two masters, one in mechanical engineering and the other in product design, she has decided to continue on for a Ph.D., researching how industrialized manufacturing techniques translate to developing countries. She now splits her time between California and Kenya, but is forever looking for a fresh audience for her Canadianisms. Please e-mail her at kmd@leland.stanford.edu if you have any comments, suggestions, or flattery.

About the Illustrator

DANIEL SUNG-HWE KIM is a full-time product design engineer and a part-time graphic designer and freelance illustrator. Originally from Seoul, Korea, Daniel holds a B.S. in Mechanical Engineering and an M.S. in Product Design from Stanford University, where he was fortunate enough to sit across from the author for a whole year. Currently, Daniel is designing very cool products at IDEO Product Development in Palo Alto, California. You can contact him at dkim@ideo.com for any questions or comments.

Index